REIGNIN(

DR DEREK STRINGER

STUDIES FROM THE OLD TESTAMENT BOOKS
OF 1 AND 2 KINGS AND SECOND CHRONICLES

The Good News Broadcasting
Association (Great Britain) Limited

Good News Broadcasting Association (UK)
Ranskill. DN22 8NN. England
Email:info@gnba.net Web site:www.gnba.net

British Library Cataloguing In Publication Data

A Record of this Publication is available from the British Library

ISBN 1846853524
978-1-84685-352-4

Published September 2006 by

Exposure Publishing, an imprint of Diggory Press,
Three Rivers, Minions, Liskeard, Cornwall, PL14 5LE, UK
WWW.DIGGORYPRESS.COM

THE BIG IDEA

During an Army war game a commanding officer's jeep got stuck in the mud. He saw some men lounging around nearby and asked them to help him get unstuck. "Sorry sir," said one of the loafers, "but we've been classified dead and the umpire said we couldn't contribute in any way." The C.O. turned to his driver and said, "Go and drag a couple of those dead bodies over here and throw them under the wheels to give us some traction".

War games are not the only places that you can see a bunch of "dead" bodies walking around. In fact, we live in a world of the "living dead". Paul wrote in Ephesians 2: 1-2a "As for you, you were dead in your transgressions and sins, in which you used to live when you followed the ways of this world . ."

Did you notice that? We were dead. This death was not a separation of the spirit from the body, but a separation from God. Thank God He will bring the dead (both spiritual and physical) back to life! And not just that. Every believer is meant to 'reign in life' (see Romans 6:12).

There is nothing written in the Old Testament that cannot help us live effective and useful Christian lives. (see Romans 15: 4 and 1 Corinthians 10: 6) Therefore, studying the Kings of 1 and 2 Kings (plus Chronicles) will give many practical lessons to help us 'king it' in life.

Let's find out how . . .

Reigning in life

Contents

Chapter 1
Solomon
A Discerning Heart

Suppose I was in a position to give you any three wishes your little heart desired, what would they be? That's right. Anything you want. Have you got it? Now just hold it in your mind; we'll come back to it.

I am excited about the theme of this book. It is based upon one of the least read portions of the Bible, the Old Testament books of 1 and 2 Kings, with supplemental material from Second Chronicles. Some people have called this "the graveyard" of the Scriptures, both figuratively because it's a place we tend to avoid, and literally because an awful lot of deaths and burials are recorded there. Over the next few chapters I want us to examine some of the tombstones in this graveyard, and particularly the epitaphs God has written on some of those tombstones. Epitaphs, you know, are often used to sum-up a person's life.

I have entitled this book, "Reigning In Life." The point is this: as leaders go, so goes a nation, or a company, or a church. We see this so clearly in the lives of the ancient Israelites. When a godly king was on the throne spiritual blessings were enjoyed. On the other hand, when a wicked ruler was in charge spiritual chaos was inevitably the result. I think that is still true today. I, for one, would rather live under the current threat of terrorism and with the economy in a decline, but with leaders who acknowledge God and try to pursue biblical standards, than to experience budget surpluses but moral deficits under leaders whose ethical standards are gleaned from opinion polls. I would also rather endure average preaching and mediocre music under Church leaders known for their integrity and pursuit of holiness than to hear brilliant and eloquent sermons and quality music produced by leaders more concerned with their own press clippings than with the Lord.

Still a question may come to your minds: "Why explore a graveyard for epitaphs when one has so many other options, like studying one of the Gospels, or one of the great New Testament epistles, or even the Book of Revelation?" My answer is found in 2 Timothy 3:16: "All Scripture is God-breathed and is useful for teaching, rebuking, correcting and training in righteousness." I take that literally – all Scripture. That's why we try at Good News Broadcasting to offer a balance between Old Testament teaching and New Testament teaching on radio, between narrative and doctrinal portions of the Bible. I believe our spiritual health depends upon a balanced diet from the Word of God.

David is the greatest king in Israel's history. To study him would take a whole book. We are going to pick up with his successor as King of Israel, namely Solomon, and then, we will consider the lives and legacies of at least 15 of the Kings of Israel and Judah. I'm fired up for this!

Before beginning our journey with Solomon, I think it would be helpful to offer a very brief overview of Jewish history so we can see how this period of the Kings fits into the whole.

The big picture

The father of the Jewish people was Abraham, who lived in the 21st century BC. He was the first of four great patriarchs – Abraham, Isaac, Jacob and Joseph – who spanned roughly 400 years. Joseph, the last of the patriarchs, was sold by his brothers into slavery in Egypt and, by God's amazing providence, eventually became the Prime Minister of Egypt. Years later, when a great famine hit the entire Middle East, Joseph's brothers went to Egypt to find food and ended up finding reconciliation with their long-lost brother, whom they presumed was dead. The Pharaoh also gave them a new home in the Nile Delta of Egypt, and this extended family of about 70 members became a nation of several million over the next 400 years. After Joseph's death another Pharaoh came to power, who didn't know Joseph, and the fortunes of the Israelites deteriorated markedly; they became slaves rather than guests.

In about the year 1446, the Israelites were rescued from Egypt by God's miraculous power.

Moses led them across the Sea of Reeds, to Mount Sinai, and then through the desert to the doorstep of the Promised Land. Tragically, the people rebelled against God and, as a result, they had to spend nearly 40 years wandering in the desert until an entire generation died off. But eventually Joshua led them across the Jordan River and into the land God had promised to Abraham some 700 years earlier.

The Conquest of the land from the pagan tribes who lived there took about 30 years, and then for about three centuries the Israelites lived in a sort of theocracy, with God ruling through a series of judges. Eventually they begged God for a king, because the other nations had one, and reluctantly God gave in to their wishes, warning them that there were grave dangers associated with centralised power. He gave them Saul as their first king, a man with great potential, but one who sadly failed to live up to his gifts and abilities. He was followed by David, and David by Solomon. This was known as the Golden Age of Israel or the United Monarchy.

The Kingdom split after the death of Solomon in 931 BC, with ten tribes forming the Nation of Israel under Jeroboam and two tribes forming the Nation of Judah under Rehoboam. Both countries largely failed to follow the Lord, though Judah, whose Kings were all descendants of David, had at least a few righteous rulers. Israel had none, and as a result, God brought the Assyrians in 722 BC to destroy their nation and carry off its inhabitants into exile. To this day they are known as the Ten Lost Tribes of Israel, for no Jewish person today can trace his or her ancestry to any of these tribes. Judah lasted for another 140 years until King Nebuchadnezzar of the Babylonians put it out of its misery in about 600 BC.

The first thing we discover in the book of 1 Kings is that . . . the torch is passed from David to Solomon.

David is very old and near death, but choosing his successor turns out to be anything but simple, for David had several wives and many children, he was not a great father, and therefore there was a lot of bad blood in the family. Bathsheba wanted her son Solomon to become King, and David had agreed, but an older son, Adonijah, had himself crowned first. However, with the help of Bathsheba, Zadok the high priest, Nathan the prophet, and a number of other loyal officials, Solomon was given the throne, Adonijah surrendered, and the Kingdom was eventually firmly established under Solomon's control.

The official passing of the torch involved a beautiful and profound charge from David to Solomon at the beginning of 1 Kings 2. "I am about to go the way of all the earth," he said. "So be strong, show yourself a man, and observe what the LORD your God requires: Walk in his ways, and keep his decrees and commands, his laws and requirements, as written in the Law of Moses, so that you may prosper in all you do and wherever you go, and that the LORD may keep His promise to me: 'If your descendants watch how they live, and if they walk faithfully before me with all their heart and soul, you will never fail to have a man on the throne of Israel.'"

The key concept David communicates here to his son and successor is the need for obedience to God's commandments. It is conveyed through such terms as "observe," "walk", "keep," and "watch." God's full blessings have always been contingent upon obedience. Not His salvation, mind you – that is based on grace. But the full realisation of joy and peace and happiness and spiritual prosperity depends upon obedience.

Solomon could have heeded that charge better than he did.

In 1 Kings 3 we read about a remarkable exchange between the Lord and Solomon. It happened through a dream, but it was nevertheless very real. In this exchange, the Lord offers to give Solomon whatever he wants. Solomon, we discover, starts out pretty well. It says in 1 Kings 3:3 that "Solomon showed his love for the Lord by walking according to the statutes of his father David, except that he offered sacrifices and burned incense on the high places."

That seems like a small exception, but it is perhaps more significant than we might first think. We will hear a lot about the high places in our study of the Kings. These were places of worship that pagans built on the top of mountains because they believed their gods were more accessible there. This doesn't mean that Solomon is himself participating in pagan worship; actually he is offering sacrifices to the Lord God, but he is doing it from pagan altars. This, in spite of the fact that God had specified that He wanted worship to take place in the tabernacle in Jerusalem, where the Ark of the Covenant resided.

Why does Solomon choose to worship at the high places instead of in the Tabernacle? I suspect it is because he is an ostentatious person; he seems to love the attention he received by sacrificing huge numbers of animals on the top of a mountain. And while God does not approve of his compromise, God is nothing if not gracious. So one night, after Solomon offered a thousand burnt offerings on the altar at the high place of Gibeon, the Lord appears to him during the night and says, "Ask for whatever you want me to give you."

I asked you earlier to think about your own wishes. How do they compare to what Solomon asked for? In verse 7 we discover that after thanking God for his kindness to David and to himself, the young king responds: "I am only a little child and do not know how to carry out my duties. Your servant is here among the people you have chosen, a great people, too numerous to count or number. So give your servant a discerning heart to govern your people and to distinguish between right and wrong." And it says, "The Lord was pleased that Solomon had asked for this." I'm going to share later that I think Solomon could have done better, but he certainly could also have done worse.

Here's how God responds to Solomon's request: "Since you have asked for this and not for long life or wealth for yourself, nor have asked for the death of your enemies but for discernment in administering justice, I will do what you have asked. I will give you a wise and discerning heart, so that there will never have been anyone like you, nor will there ever be. Moreover, I will give you what you have not asked for – both riches and honour – so that in your lifetime you will have no equal among kings. And if you walk in my ways and obey my statutes and commands as David your father did, I will give you a long life."

Let's stop here and think for a moment about what wisdom is.

We can define wisdom this way: "Wisdom is the capacity to see things from God's perspective and to respond to them according to Scriptural principles." Another way of stating the same thing is that "Wisdom is seeking heavenly opinions on earthly circumstances."

Wisdom is not just knowledge, though wisdom employs knowledge. Actually some of the most knowledgeable, brilliant people on earth are fools, not wise, by God's standards. Leading universities may have the greatest concentration of brainpower per capita on the face of the earth, but wisdom is in extremely short supply. That's why so many intelligent people mess-up their lives. Wisdom starts and ends with God. Proverbs 9:10 says, "The fear of the Lord is the beginning of wisdom, and knowledge of the Holy One is understanding." "Fear" here means reverence or awe. True wisdom and discernment is what Solomon sought, and this is what God grants him, with the result that . . . Solomon receives wisdom greater than that of all other kings of the earth.

The writer offers us an illustration of Solomon's wisdom by means of a true story, found in 1 Kings 3:16. Two women lived in the same house and each had a baby, just three days apart. A short time later, the one woman smothered her son accidentally during the night. So, she got up and switched babies with the other woman, who was still sleeping. When this other woman woke up to nurse her son, she was stunned to find him dead, but on closer examination, her motherly instincts told her the dead child was not hers. But she could not prove it; there were no witnesses, there were no DNA tests to confirm it, and, perhaps because they were both prostitutes, no one cared to bring the matter to justice. The issue eventually came to the attention of Solomon.

We pick up the story in verse 23. The King said, "This one says, 'My son is alive and your son is dead,' while that one says, 'No! Your son is dead and mine is alive.'" Then the King said, "Bring me a sword." So they brought a sword for the king. He then gave an Order: "Cut the living child in two and give half to one and half to the other." The woman whose son was alive was filled with compassion for her son and said to the King, "Please, my lord, give her the living baby! Don't kill him!" But the other said, "Neither I nor you shall have him. Cut him in two!" Then the King gave his ruling: "Give the living baby to the first woman. Do not kill him; she is his mother." When all Israel heard the verdict the King had given, they held the King in awe, because they saw that he had wisdom from God to administer justice.

Just how great was Solomon's wisdom?

We read in I Kings 4:29 that . . . "God gave Solomon wisdom and very great insight, and a breadth of understanding as measureless as the sand on the seashore. Solomon's wisdom was greater than the wisdom of all the men of the East, and greater than all the wisdom of Egypt. He was wiser than any other man . . . And his fame spread to all the surrounding nations".

The writer goes on to tell us that Solomon spoke 3000 proverbs and wrote over 1000 songs. He understood plant life and taught about animals, birds, reptiles and fish. Legend tells us he was able to talk to the animals, but there's nothing in the text about that. Clearly, however, Solomon's wisdom went beyond discernment and extended to immense knowledge about a vast number of subjects.

In Chapter 10 we have the fascinating story of the visit of the Queen of Sheba. She came in order to test Solomon with hard questions, and he answered all her questions – nothing was too hard for the king to explain. Here's her reaction in her own words: "The report I heard in my own country about your achievements and your wisdom is true. But I did not believe these things until I came and saw with my own eyes. Indeed, not even half was told me." But you will recall that God not only granted Solomon what he requested, but He also gave him what he did not request, namely wealth – probably just God's gracious way of rewarding him for his unselfishness.

Solomon also receives riches greater than that of all other kings of the earth.

Just how rich was he? In Chapter 4 we are told that he had 4000 stalls for chariot horses, and 12,000 horses. In chapters 5 and following, we are told about the temple he built in Jerusalem. It was probably the most expensive building ever erected on the face of the earth, with estimates of its cost ranging from £1 billion to £12 billion. The King imported on average 25 tons of gold a year, and virtually everything in his palace was made of gold. It specifically says in I Kings 10:21 "Nothing was made of silver, because silver was considered of little value in Solomon's days." And a few verses later it adds, "The King made silver as common in Jerusalem as stones and cedar as plentiful as sycamore-fig trees." Further it says in verse 22 that "The King had a fleet of trading ships at sea . . . Once every three years it returned, carrying gold, silver and ivory, and apes and baboons."

Look at the summary of both his wisdom and his wealth in I Kings 10:23-25: "King Solomon was greater in riches and wisdom than all the other kings of the earth. The whole world sought audience with Solomon to hear the wisdom God had put in his heart. Year after year, everyone who came brought a gift – articles of silver and gold, robes, weapons and spices, and horses and mules." But, there is another message in this amazing account, and that is that wisdom and riches are not enough – not enough to produce spiritual success.

Do not misunderstand me. God given wisdom or discernment is a great gift and is to be envied. Over the years I have come to believe that the most important gift for a leader in God's church is the gift of discernment. Oh, I know we need a balance of gifts, including administration and leadership and mercy (we need them all), but without a strong dose of discernment among the leaders of God's church, the best of intentions will fall short.

Wealth is also a good gift from God, though there is a great deal more risk associated with it. The options that wealthy people have for serving the Lord and accomplishing good for mankind are enormous. But, neither wisdom nor wealth can produce spiritual success in and of themselves. Solomon had both but they were not well balanced with obedience, with the result that Solomon was largely a spiritual failure. The very first thing we are told about Solomon after the consolidation of his Kingdom is this: "Solomon made an alliance with Pharaoh King of Egypt and married his daughter." God had made it clear that he didn't want his people to be making political alliances to protect themselves– He wanted them to rely on Him. But Solomon disobeyed and when Solomon disobeyed, he did it in style.

In Chapter 11 we read: "King Solomon, however, loved many foreign women besides Pharaoh's daughter . . . They were from nations about which the LORD had told the Israelites, 'You must not intermarry with them, because they will surely turn your hearts after their gods.' Nevertheless, Solomon held fast to them in love. He had seven hundred wives of royal birth and three hundred concubines, and his wives led him astray. As Solomon grew old, his wives turned his heart after other gods, and his heart was not fully devoted to the LORD his God, as the heart of David his father had been."

Some commentators see a contradiction here between Solomon's wisdom and his actions.

Anyone who would take on a thousand mothers-in-law cannot be exceptionally bright. (Just kidding, I have a wonderful mother-in-law). Seriously, I think what we see here in Solomon is the plague of a divided heart; he had other loves, and those loves drew him away from the Lord. Solomon is so much like us when we passionately express our love for the Lord and yet have divided hearts. I think of the businessman who professes strong faith in Christ, yet tolerates unethical practices in his business. I think of the husband who loves his wife yet has a secret habit with pornography. I think of anyone of us who worships and praises the Lord but clings to something God has forbidden.

A pastor tells about rounding the corner of his house one day to find his 3-year-old son wrestling with the family's Labrador retriever. The boy had a bear hug on the dog's mid-section, his face pressed right into her side. The dog was known to put up with this for a while, but when she finally had enough, she would turn around and nip him. The little boy knew that, but he was stubborn. This particular time, unaware of his dad approaching, he was squeezing the dog with his eyes shut, all the while praying out loud, "Dear God, please don't let the dog bite me!" His dad interrupted him, "Hey, I think God is more likely to answer that prayer if you let go of the dog."

We are so much that way. We cling to something we know is going to hurt us, and we plead, "Lord, don't let it bite us!" We say, "Lord, I love you, but I love something else, too. It is so very important to me and I have to cling to it." Perhaps it is a relationship we know is wrong. Maybe it is some habit we know is going to produce harmful consequences. Perhaps it is even something that is good but not the best. Solomon's problem was that he had a divided heart, and it eventually led to his downfall.

I want us to ponder the truths we need to take home from this portion of Solomon's life.

1. Wisdom is no substitute for obedience

There is a very profound verse in 1 Samuel 15:22 which it would do us well to have emblazoned on our hearts and minds. King Saul was in battle against the Amalekites. The prophet Samuel had given him a message from the Lord to the effect that he was to destroy everything that belonged to this enemy. But Saul relied on his own reasoning and spared the best of the sheep and cattle in order to offer a sacrifice to God. Here is how Samuel responds: "Does the Lord delight in burnt offerings and sacrifices as much as in obeying the voice of the Lord? To obey is better than sacrifice, and to heed is better than the fat of rams."

You may be brilliant; you may have reasoning powers that enable you to win any argument; you may even have the gifts of discernment and wisdom and knowledge. But none of that is a substitute for obedience to God. You may not feel very intelligent yourself. You may not think you are very competent. You may consider yourself a failure. But you can live a full and rich life and one that is pleasing to God if you are simply obedient. It's not an issue of native ability; it's an issue of humility and surrender to the Lordship of Christ.

2. Wisdom is no substitute for proper priorities

Solomon took seven years building the Temple. It took Solomon thirteen years, however, to complete the construction of his palace. The great Temple of Solomon served as the centre of Jewish worship for between 300 and 400 years until King Nebuchadnezzar tore it down. It was the culmination of a dream God gave to David years before. Solomon did a wonderful job building it, but he spent nearly twice as long building his own personal palace as he did that great Temple. I would say his priorities were out of order.

I wonder if Solomon's personal priorities weren't out of order even when he made his famous request of God. Remember exactly what he asked for back in Chapter 3? "So give your servant a discerning heart to govern your people and to distinguish between right and wrong. For who is able to govern this great people of yours?" This was a good request, but it was probably not the best one he could have made. His focus was on wisdom for governing the nation; what he lacked was wisdom to govern his own life. Wisdom is no substitute for proper priorities.

God wants us to put first things first in our lives. We can be hugely successful in our careers, but if we have to relegate God to a distant place in order to accomplish that, we have failed miserably. We may be hugely successful in ministry, but if our families are in disarray as a result, we have failed miserably. We may be very knowledgeable in this area or that, but if we haven't learned how to "see things in our own lives from God's perspective and to respond to them according to biblical principles," we will fail miserably.

3. Wisdom is no substitute for intimacy with the Lord.

It is difficult not to draw some comparisons between David and Solomon. They were both monumental figures in Israel's history. On the scale of political ability, Solomon outdid his father, as he consolidated his Kingdom and enjoyed an unbroken time of peace. Both men were extremely wealthy, but Solomon again outstripped his father. In regard to territory, Solomon certainly had more influence and power. Yet, when you look at their legacies, David comes out way ahead. Solomon virtually disappears from view once he dies, while David is mentioned in almost every book of the Bible.

Again and again God says, "For David's sake" I will do such and such. "For David's sake" I will refrain from such-and-such. Why? Well, David was no less a sinner than Solomon, but he had an unsurpassed love for the Lord. He was a man after God's own heart. Great sin can be resolved by great forgiveness, but a divided heart is always fatal. Whether or not God ever asked David verbally what he desired above all other things, as He did Solomon, and as I asked all of us earlier, David tells us what his answer would have been. In Psalm 27:4 he writes, "One thing I have asked from the Lord, that I shall seek; That I may dwell in the House of the Lord all the days of my life, To behold the beauty of the Lord, And to meditate in His temple." Solomon sought discernment from the Lord to rule his country; David sought the Lord.

None of us will ever match Solomon in wisdom and discernment (God specifically promised that there would never be anyone like Solomon). But wisdom is something he desires each of us to pursue. Later in his life Solomon wrote most of the Book of Proverbs, and the first four chapters are devoted completely to extolling wisdom.

I think God wants each of us to pray Solomon's prayer: "Give your servant a discerning heart," the capacity to see things from God's perspective and to respond to them according to Scriptural principles. But he wants even more for us to seek intimacy with Him.

Chapter 2
Solomon
Great Achievements

An ice-breaker at a seminar was, "If you had a choice of all human beings, dead or alive, with whom would you choose to spend an afternoon?" It was fascinating to hear the answers and the reasons for the answers.

If someone were to ask me, "What building, present or past, would you like to visit," I would be quick to answer – Solomon's Temple. It was not a particularly large building, but it was probably the most costly one ever constructed on planet earth. The mythical King Croesus would have envied the gold found in Solomon's masterpiece. The Temple was the centre of Jewish worship for between 300 and 400 years, and then after being destroyed, it was rebuilt and remained the centre of worship for another 600 years. One cannot really understand the sacrificial system that provided atonement for sin in the Old Testament without understanding the Temple and its predecessor, the Tabernacle. I would love to see it in person.

In our first chapter we began examining the epitaphs on various tombstones in the graveyard of the Kings and prophets of Israel, beginning with Solomon. One of the key issues we are looking for in Kings and Chronicles is how leaders set the standard for the people of

God. Leaders have such a huge capacity for good or ill.

This is true even today, despite the fact that we live in a day and time when leadership has taken some huge hits. The result is that a lot of people are searching for answers anywhere they can find them – in their own inner selves, in psychic mediums, in false religions, and in all kinds of radical movements. Yet I believe people really want to be led, and they will follow leaders who are authentic and who exhibit integrity.

Christians are called to 'reign in life'. In other words we should 'King it', not be reigned over by life, but give it some leadership. And we can learn by way of example from the Kings and leaders of Old Testament days. That makes our Bible study very relevant.

The leader who gets the most press in 1 Kings is Solomon. The two events that define him more than any others, and therefore provide effective epitaphs for him, are first his request for wisdom and second his building of the Temple in Jerusalem.

In Chapter One we considered the first event, as Solomon said to the Lord: "Give me a discerning heart." Now we look at the second, using once again a quotation from Solomon's own lips: "I intend to build a temple for the name of the Lord my God." This quotation comes directly from a letter he wrote to Hiram King of Tyre in 1 Kings

5:3. There is little doubt this was Solomon's greatest achievement: A temple for the Lord. The temple was such a monumental building, both in cost and function, that I think it would be well for us to try to grasp the scope of it by considering a number of factors that were involved in its completion.

Let's begin with the dream that preceded the reality

The notion of building a temple was not originally Solomon's. King David had it in his heart for a long time to build a permanent home for the Ark of the Covenant, a place where God could dwell among His people. In fact, long before Solomon was even born, David made a proposal to build a temple and revealed his motive for it: "After David was settled in his palace, he said to Nathan the prophet, 'Here I am, living in a palace of cedar, while the ark of the covenant of the LORD is under a tent.' Nathan replied to David, 'Whatever you have in mind, do it, for God is with you.'"

David was feeling guilt, probably legitimate guilt, over the fact that he was living in a luxurious palace while the Lord's House was essentially a temporary tent. However, the same night the Word of the Lord came to the prophet Nathan informing him that David was not to build the temple because he had shed much blood and fought many wars. God offered instead to give David a son who would be a man of peace and rest. In fact, his name would mean peace, Shalom or Solomon. He would be the one to build a House for God. David speaks of the purpose for a temple in 1 Chronicles chapter 29, where he commissions Solomon to build it: "Then King David said to the whole assembly: 'My son Solomon, the one whom God has chosen, is young and inexperienced. The task is great, because this palatial structure is not for man but for the Lord God.'"

The temple was not a man-centred project (in fact, only the priests could even enter the main building) but a God-centred one. Its primary purpose was to reveal the awesome majesty of God, and to serve as a place to confess sin, offer sacrifice, and receive atonement. Even the architecture of the building drew everyone's attention to the attributes of God. The gold and precious stones spoke of His majesty and splendour. The Holy of Holies spoke of His holiness. The Ark of the Covenant spoke of His mercy. The altar spoke of God's atonement for man's sin. The whole temple spoke of His sovereignty. Its purpose was to be a House for God.

It is important for us to realise that not every house of worship is built for God; in fact, I would suggest that most church buildings today are constructed almost exclusively for people. The issues that drive the architects are comfort, utility, and ease of access, safety, recreation, and fellowship (horizontal). The latest fads in churches are food courts and indoor playgrounds. Now please don't misunderstand me; I'm not necessarily criticising these developments. In fact, I tend to feel it is a mistake when church buildings are patterned after the architecture of the Temple. Everything changed dramatically with the death of Christ. I will return to this topic later.

Again we have to go back to King David for the plans, for it says in I Kings 28:11, "Then David gave his son Solomon the plans for the portico of the temple, its buildings, its storerooms, its upper parts, its inner rooms and the place of atonement. He gave him the plans of all that the Spirit had put in his mind . . . " The same passage goes on to describe in detail the construction and the furnishings of the temple. Then in verse 19 we read, "All this," David said, "I have in writing from the hand of the Lord upon me, and he gave me understanding in all the details of the plan." In other words, the plans were revealed by God Himself, and therefore any human criticism of the temple must be directed at its divine Architect. Clearly, God is not fundamentally opposed to beauty or even luxury. (I have often thought it would be nice if God would provide plans for our church buildings today. We could not only save substantially on architectural fees, but we could also avoid all the disagreements that go with trying to decide the issues ourselves. Pews or chairs? Just check with God. Unfortunately, God has left such decisions up to us).

The building project David was launching had a pretty serious price tag. Most estimates I've read of the cost of the Solomon's Temple in today's money are in the multiple billions. Probably no other building in the history of mankind had more gold in it than this one. Talk about a fund-raising effort! Actually, David's stewardship plan was pretty simple and extremely effective.

First, he gave generously from the government coffers. In those days there was no separation of church and state, so taxes were readily used to fund the temple.

Then David made a lavish commitment from his own personal wealth to the tune of 110 tons of gold and 260 tons of silver.

Third, the leaders declared their own commitment and sacrifice, and they actually out-gave David as a group (190 tons of gold, 375 tons of silver, 675 tons of bronze, 3,750 tons of iron (which was much more rare and therefore more valuable than it is today), plus an unspecified number of precious stones.

And finally, the common people followed joyfully and willingly. It was an amazing display of generous giving. 1 Kings Chapter 5 is entirely devoted to the preparations for the building of the temple, that's the collection of materials and human resources. Solomon ordered the wood from Lebanon, known for its great cedars. Hiram King of Tyre agreed to provide logs, move them to the Mediterranean, and float them down to Israel, all in exchange for food for his royal household.

The work on the logs was actually done by conscripted labourers from Israel – 30,000 of them. They rotated, with 10,000 working in Lebanon for a month at a time, while 20,000 spent two months at home, but still working on the Temple project. Solomon also had 80,000 stonecutters who cut the large blocks for the foundation of the temple. I have seen with my own eyes the quality of work that they did. Twenty feet below the Wailing Wall in Jerusalem, in a tunnel only unearthed in the past 20 years or so, one can see some of the original foundation stones of Solomon's temple. Nearly 3,000 years later these stones the size of a pick-up truck still fit together perfectly, without any mortar to hold them together.

In 1 Kings 6 we learn that Solomon started the building in his fourth year, 966 BC. We are also told the size of the main part of the temple, about 90 feet long, 30 feet wide, and 45 feet high. We're not talking huge here. The main building of the Temple would easily fit into a school sports hall, except that it would stick out through the roof a little. The Temple had two main rooms, a Most Holy Place that was a 30-foot cube (apparently with an attic over it) and the Holy Place that was 60 feet by 30 feet by 45 feet high. The inside of the temple was cedar, carved with gourds, palm trees, and open flowers, but then the cedar was all overlaid with pure gold. The floors and ceilings were also covered with gold. In addition to the main building, there was a portico, or porch at the front that extended another 15 feet, plus a structure around the building that provided three floors of side rooms. There were also courts outside that allowed the common people to gather, though they could not enter the main building.

Most of the seventh chapter is devoted to the furnishings. The chief craftsman was Hiram of Tyre, a master craftsman in bronze. We don't have time to consider the details that are given to us, but we can look at the results. It says in 1 Kings 7:40: "So Hiram finished all the work he had undertaken for King Solomon in the temple of the LORD: the two pillars; the two bowl-shaped capitals on top of the pillars; the two sets of network decorating the two bowl-shaped capitals on top of the pillars; the four hundred pomegranates for the two sets of network (two rows of pomegranates for each network, decorating the bowl-shaped capitals on top of the pillars); the ten stands with their ten basins; the Sea and the twelve bulls under it; the pots, shovels and sprinkling bowls. All these objects that Hiram made for King Solomon for the temple of the LORD were of burnished bronze."

Then in verse 48 we read about additional furnishings made of gold. "Solomon also made all the furnishings that were in the Lord's temple: the golden altar; the golden table on which was the bread of the Presence; the lamp stands of pure gold (five on the right and five on the left, in front of the inner sanctuary); the gold floral work and lamps and tongs; the pure gold basins, wick trimmers, sprinkling bowls, dishes and censers; and the gold sockets for the doors of the innermost room, the Most Holy Place, and also for the doors of the main hall of the temple."

By the way, it has been argued convincingly that in ancient Jewish tradition the open flowers, palm trees and pomegranates in the temple were taken to be reminiscent of the Garden of Eden. In addition the entrances to both the Temple and the Garden were on the East. The Temple was viewed as a place where God would dwell with his people, just as he dwelt with Adam and Eve before the Fall.

In Chapter 8 we learn of the move of the Ark of the Covenant to the Temple. The Ark had been constructed by Moses. It was the most sacred object in Israel, representing the very presence of the Lord, and there were tight restrictions as to how it should be handled and where it should reside. Originally the Ark contained the stone tablets on which God had written the Ten Commandments, samples of the manna that God provided from Heaven, and Aaron's rod that budded at the time of Korah's rebellion, but according to 1 Kings 8:9, nothing was in it now except the two stone tablets.

In a dramatic ceremony the Ark was moved from the Tabernacle to the Temple. It was placed in the Holy of Holies, or the Most Holy Place, beneath the wings of the golden cherubim. When the priests withdrew from the Holy Place, the glory of the Lord filled the temple in the form of a cloud so that the priests could not even do their work. There are a lot of myths in the movie, "Raiders of the Lost Ark," but clearly there was something unique about that little box. 1 Kings 8 contains the longest prayer in the Bible – it is Solomon's Prayer at the Dedication of the Temple. This magnificent prayer contains both adoration and supplication, and it is followed by unprecedented celebration.

Think about these words spoken by the King as he stood before the altar of the Lord in front of the whole assembly of Israel, with his hands spread toward the heavens: "O LORD, God of Israel, there is no God like you in Heaven above or on earth below – you who keep your covenant of love with your servants who continue wholeheartedly in your way. You have kept your promise to your servant David my father; with your mouth you have promised and with your hand you have fulfilled it – as it is today. But will God really dwell on earth? The heavens, even the highest heaven, cannot contain you. How much less this temple I have built!"

Solomon recognised that while this Temple was a building for God, it could not contain God. While it was a place where His presence would be uniquely experienced, God was far too great to be limited to one place, as the pagan gods were. Solomon first and foremost desired to express adoration for this great God! Solomon moves quickly from adoring God to laying requests before Him, but they are not the typical requests we so often offer up for health or healing, for employment or travelling mercies. They are spiritual requests, especially for forgiveness.

Beginning in verse 28: “Yet give attention to your servant’s prayer and his plea for mercy, O LORD my God. Hear the cry and the prayer that your servant is praying in your presence this day. May your eyes be open toward this temple night and day, this place of which you said, ‘My Name shall be there,’ so that you will hear the prayer your servant prays toward this place. Hear the supplication of your servant and of your people Israel when they pray toward this place. Hear from Heaven, your dwelling place, and when you hear, forgive.”

Solomon then expands upon the need for mercy by going through a whole litany of potential spiritual failures and natural disasters, asking God in each case to hear from Heaven and act on behalf of His people. Among the failures and disasters he mentions are these actions:

When a man wrongs his neighbour . . .

When your people Israel have been defeated by an enemy because they have sinned against you . . .

When the heavens are shut up and there is no rain because your people have sinned against you . . .

When famine or plague comes to the land . . .

When your people go to war against their enemies . . .

When they sin against you . . . and they end up captives near or far . . .

In each case Solomon begs God to hear when the people turn back to Him and confess their sins. He knows that repentance and a change of heart are prerequisites to God's healing and restoration. But once they have repented, Solomon is not hesitant to ask for God's forgiveness.

Nor is Solomon's prayer selfish – focused only on Israel and its welfare. He was also aware that God had a great love for the nations. Read verses 41-43: "As for the foreigner who does not belong to your people Israel, but has come from a distant land because of your Name – for men will hear of your great Name and your mighty hand and your outstretched arm – when he comes and prays toward this temple, then hear from Heaven, your dwelling place, and do whatever the foreigner asks of you, so that all the peoples of the earth may know your Name and fear you, as do your own people Israel, and may know that this House I have built bears your Name."

Solomon puts his money where his mouth is in the dedication ceremony. He offers 22,000 cattle and 120,000 sheep and goats as burnt offerings to the Lord. The celebration lasts for 14 full days. Then the people go home, "joyful and glad in heart" for all the good things the Lord had done for them.

God appears to Solomon in 1 Kings 9:3 and says, "I have heard the prayer and plea you have made before me; I have consecrated this temple, which you have built, by putting my Name there forever. My eyes and my heart will always be there."

Any notion that this Temple was a mistake, a waste of money that could have been better spent on the poor, goes out the window with God's acceptance of it as a place where He chooses to dwell.

He offers conditional promises to His people. A conditional promise is one of the "if . . . then" variety. If you will do this, then I will do that. Consider what God says from 2 Chronicles 7 (it's talking about the same event as 1 Kings 9, but the wording is a little more familiar to us): "When I shut up the heavens so that there is no rain, or command locusts to devour the land or send a plague among my people, if my people, who are called by my name, will humble themselves and pray and seek my face and turn from their wicked ways, then will I hear from

Heaven and will forgive their sin and will heal their land."

I struggle with how applicable this well-known promise is to us today. It was clearly directed to Israel as a promise to heal their land when they repented. But I tend to feel there is a principle here that applies across the centuries and across geographical boundaries. Whenever God's people are suffering because of sin, if they will humble themselves and pray and repent, God will hear from Heaven and forgive them. That may not always be demonstrated in physical deliverance, but it is at least a promise of spiritual deliverance.

Do you know what happened to the temple?

It was destroyed by King Nebuchadnezzar of Babylon. Nebuchadnezzar came against Judah three times. In 606 BC he took a number of hostages, including four young Jewish men: Daniel, Shadrach, Meshach, and Abednego. He came back in 598, seizing thousands of additional captives and carrying off all the articles from the temple, both large and small. And he came back a final time in 586, burning the temple, breaking down the wall of Jerusalem, and totally destroying everything of value.

Jerusalem was rebuilt and expanded, before it was destroyed again by the Roman Emperor Titus. You can read about the rebuilding of the Temple in the book of Ezra and in the prophet

Haggai. Actually, the poverty-stricken exiles who returned from the Babylonian captivity to rebuild the Temple in 516 B.C., could do little more than build a log-cabin replica on the original foundation. In fact, in the second chapter of Haggai we learn that the rebuilt temple "looked like nothing" to those who saw the temple in its former glory. But God told them not to fear, that His Spirit remained with them. In fact, God promised, "I will fill this House with glory." Not only that, "'The glory of this present House will be greater than the glory of the former House,' says the Lord Almighty. 'And in this place I will grant peace,' declares the Lord Almighty."

Amazing, does he really mean it? Greater than the glory of Solomon's temple? Clearly this prophecy of a greater glory refers to something other than gold and silver; I believe it is speaking of the glory that was present in the rebuilt temple because Jesus walked and taught there. If the Temple symbolised the dwelling of God with His people, then the glory of Solomon's Temple was far exceeded when the Glorious One, Jesus Christ, came and "tabernacled" or "templed" among us.

The rebuilt Temple of the Exiles was expanded and refurbished in a major way by King Herod. You may recall that Jesus once challenged the Jews, "Destroy this temple, and I will raise it again in three days." The Jews replied, "It has taken forty-six years to build this temple, and you are going to raise it in three days?" Jesus, of course, was speaking figuratively of His own death and resurrection, but clearly the temple was in the middle of a major renovation, work that continued for several decades after Christ. It was once again a magnificent structure, actually larger than the Solomon version but minus most of the gold.

Tragically, Herod's temple was destroyed in AD 70, just six years after it was finished, as the Roman Emperor Titus came and levelled Jerusalem either killing its inhabitants or taking them captive. This time the exile of the Jews from their Promised Land was not for 70 years but for nearly 19 centuries. Israel did not exist again as a nation from AD 70 until AD 1948. And even today a mosque sits on the foundation of Solomon's temple.

We have seen that the Temple was destroyed by Nebuchadnezzar and destroyed again by the Romans. Humanly speaking those were tragedies, but God was working His perfect plan through it all. It was replaced by the temple of the Holy Spirit – the Body of Christ and the body of the true believer. Let me mention several reasons why I believe this.

First, there is no evidence of a focus on buildings in the New Testament; in fact, there is not a single statement in the New Testament encouraging Christians to erect buildings. Yes, the early disciples worshiped at the temple, and Paul regularly went to the Jewish synagogues in whatever city he visited, but the reason is because that is where the religious people could be found. If Jews were to be confronted with their need for Messiah Jesus, the best place to find them was in the temple and in synagogues. But rather than using a special building, early Christian worship after the time of Christ took place primarily in homes.

Second, there are two very important passages in 1 Corinthians that identify the Temple of the Holy Spirit – and neither is talking about a building. In I Corinthians 3:16 the Apostle Paul asks this question: "Don't you know that you yourselves are God's temple and that God's Spirit lives in you? If anyone destroys God's temple, God will destroy him; for God's temple is sacred, and you are that temple." From the context and the vocabulary it is clear that Paul is talking about the local assembly of believers here as a temple. Later on in Ephesians he elaborates on this concept of the church as a temple, calling us . . . "members of God's household, built on the foundation of the apostles and prophets, with Christ Jesus himself as the chief cornerstone. In him the whole building is joined together and rises to become a holy temple in the Lord. And in him you too are being built together to become a dwelling in which God lives by his Spirit."

But it is not only the gathering of believers that is viewed as a temple in the New Testament. In 1 Corinthians 6, Paul makes a nearly identical statement about the individual believer: "Do you not know that your body is a temple of the Holy

Spirit, who is in you, whom you have received from God? You are not your own; you were bought at a price. Therefore honour God with your body." Here it is clear that Paul is talking about the believer's body, rather than the church, as a temple of the Holy Spirit.

Since I believe the Temple of Solomon has, in the providence of God, been replaced by both our corporate and individual temples, I see no reason for us to copy Solomon's Temple in our church architecture today. I believe we have great freedom to build our gathering places for worship in a way that meets our individual needs.

Yet at the same time there are lessons we can learn from the temple that apply to both our corporate and individual bodies.

One is **sacredness**

God really does dwell with us and within us, and He desires to fill us with His glory; therefore we must not treat our gatherings or our bodies with disrespect or irreverence or neglect.

Another is **holiness**

Almighty God hates sin; He cannot stand to have sin in His presence; therefore we must not tolerate sinful attitudes and sinful actions, either in our churches or in our private lives.

And a third is **forgiveness**

Just as God provided for the atonement for Israel's sins through blood sacrifice in Solomon's Temple, so today he provides for final forgiveness of our sins through the shed blood of His Son, Jesus Christ.

What a challenge to allow God to employ His enormous architectural skill to fashion our corporate fellowship and our individual bodies into a temple far more glorious than the one Solomon built, one destined to last for eternity.

How about it? An amazing truth. We are the Temple of God today. Let's be the kind of home He likes to live in.

Chapter 3
Rehoboam
Rejecting Advice

"Good friend for Jesus' sake forbear
To dig the dust enclosed here.
Blest be the man that spares these stones
And cursed be he that moves my bones."

You may recognise that as a famous epitaph coming from William Shakespeare. This one is from Winston Churchill: "I am ready to meet my Maker. Whether my Maker is prepared for the great ordeal of meeting me is another matter." I guess that Winston has gathered by now that His Maker is always ready!

I'm beginning like this because we are continuing to travel back in time into the Old Testament and the Book of Kings. We are asked as believer's today to 'reign in life' . . . The story of Old Testament Kings has a lot to teach us by way of example.

The king we look at now goes by the name of Rehoboam. I've never met someone with the name 'Rehoboam'. The Rehoboam in 1 Kings has a lot to teach us.

The Scriptures offer two powerful epitaphs for Rehoboam, and they are closely related to one another. I have chosen the first, from 1 Kings 12:8, as my title, namely, "He rejected the advice the Elders gave." But the second, from 2 Chronicles 12:14, is just as important: "He did evil because he had not set his heart on seeking the Lord." The first is outward while the second is inward. The first deals with symptoms while the second describes the disease that brought him down. Symptoms are important to understand and treat, but unless we get at the root cause, we may never do anything more than put a bandage on cancer.

Let's get the historical background

Jeroboam rebels against Solomon. In 1 Kings 11:26 we meet for the first time this very central figure in the Old Testament, a man named Jeroboam. He is mentioned 95 times in seven Old Testament books, and he himself bears one of the saddest epitaphs in the Bible: "He made Israel to sin." He is introduced here this way: "Jeroboam son of Nebat rebelled against the king. He was one of Solomon's officials." The passage goes on to tell us that Jeroboam was one of the managers of Solomon's labour force, and he got Solomon's attention through the outstanding work he did.

One day Jeroboam was on his way out of the City of Jerusalem when he was confronted by a prophet of God from Shiloh named Ahijah. As they stood alone out in the country, Ahijah took off the new coat he was wearing, tore it into twelve pieces, and told Jeroboam to take ten of the pieces for himself. Ahijah then told him the purpose of this little object lesson: God was going to tear the Kingdom of Solomon apart and give ten of the twelve tribes to Jeroboam.

The reason for this drastic action was that Israel had forsaken God and worshiped idols. Ahijah also made it clear that this division of the Kingdom would not happen as long as Solomon was living, but it would take place soon after his death.

The very next thing we read is that "Solomon tried to kill Jeroboam, but Jeroboam fled to Egypt, to Shishak the King, and stayed there until Solomon's death."

How did Jeroboam go from being a trusted official of Solomon to having a contract put out on his life? Apparently Jeroboam told someone about the message of the prophet Ahijah, the word got back to Solomon, and immediately he became suspicious. He did his best to interfere with God's plan by trying to kill Jeroboam, but to no avail. Instead Solomon himself dies, after reigning over all Israel for forty years, and Rehoboam his son succeeds him as king.

Rehoboam is crowned as Solomon's successor. At the beginning of 1 Kings 12 Rehoboam goes to Shechem to be crowned. The Israelites all come together there for the coronation, but they also make a request of their new King. Sadly, in this his first major decision as King he demonstrates serious symptoms of spiritual failure. Rehoboam rejected the advice the elders gave him in lieu of the advice of the young men.

He is approached with a reasonable request and a conditional promise. Look at 1 Kings 12: 3, 4: "So they sent for Jeroboam (who had returned from Egypt upon hearing of Solomon's death), and he and the whole assembly of Israel went to Rehoboam and said to him: "Your father put a heavy yoke on us, but now lighten the harsh labour and the heavy yoke he put on us, and we will serve you." Rehoboam answered, 'Go away for three days and then come back to me.' So the people went away."

Solomon, you will recall, was one of the wealthiest monarchs in human history. Unfortunately, all of that wealth was not rightfully gained. Much of it came from excessive taxes and forced labour. I suspect Solomon found so much fulfilment in the accolades he received for building the Temple, that when he finished that project he kept right on building. He built his own palace, then palaces and temples for many of his foreign wives, plus public works projects all over Israel. This required tremendous expenditures from the public treasury, and the only way to replenish the treasury was through higher and higher taxes.

So the people ask Rehoboam to change his father's policies and to reduce the harsh labour and heavy taxation. They don't ask for the cessation of taxes or make any other unreasonable demands. They simply ask him to lighten the load. And furthermore, they promise to serve him if he will accede to their wishes.

At first we are encouraged when we see that Rehoboam seeks advice before responding. He consults with both the elders and the young men but receives starkly conflicting advice.

Let's pick up the account in I Kings 12: 6. "Then King Rehoboam consulted the elders who had served his father Solomon during his lifetime. "How would you advise me to answer these people?" he asked. They replied, "If today you will be a servant to these people and serve them and give them a favourable answer, they will always be your servants." But Rehoboam rejected the advice the elders gave him and consulted the young men who had grown up with him and were serving him. He asked them, "What is your advice? How should we answer these people who say to me, 'Lighten the yoke your father put on us'?" The young men who had grown up with him replied, "Tell these people who have said to you, 'Your father put a heavy yoke on us, but make our yoke lighter' – tell them, 'My little finger is thicker than my father's waist. My father laid on you a heavy yoke; I will make it even heavier. My father scourged you with whips; I will scourge you with scorpions.'"

Do you notice something here? He rejects the advice of the elders even before he consults with the younger men. It's as though the moment he hears the words "servant" and "serve," he immediately decides against their advice. After all, he is the king and they are the subjects. Kings rule and subjects serve.

Sadly, that's the way a lot of people think when they get into a position of authority. But it's not how Jesus viewed authority. Do you remember what He said when confronted with the request from James and John to sit at His right and left hand in the kingdom? "Whoever wants to become great among you must be your servant, and whoever wants to be first must be your slave – just as the Son of Man did not come to be served, but to serve, and to give His life as a ransom for many."

Jesus says that the way up is down. How do you lead the people God has put under you? Maybe it's only your children. Maybe it's a small group. On the other hand, perhaps you are the leader of hundreds or thousands. It doesn't matter. All godly leadership is servant leadership. But Rehoboam has never seen that modelled and he isn't about to break the mould.

So he turns to the young men. Please understand that the young men mentioned here are not teenagers. They are Rehoboam's peers – guys he grew up with – and he is 41 years old when he becomes king! Some of you are delighted to hear that at 40 the Bible still considers you young! These forty-some-things are undoubtedly tired of the fact that Solomon and his peers – probably guys my age – have been calling the shots for a long time. The younger men view Solomon's peers as geezers who don't understand how times have changed. Now it's their turn. They have lots of ideas they wish to see fulfilled that can only be fulfilled through power and influence and money. Centralise the power! Raise the taxes! The government knows best. I will resist the temptation to draw any modern parallels.

So Rehoboam makes a momentous decision that results in the loss of most of his Kingdom. "When the people returned three days later for his answer, Rehoboam . . . followed the advice of the young men and said, "My father made your yoke heavy; I will make it even heavier. My father scourged you with whips; I will scourge you with scorpions." (Scorpions refers to whips with bits of metal imbedded in the cords). So the King did not listen to the people, for this turn of events was from the LORD, to fulfil the Word the LORD had spoken to Jeroboam son of Nebat through Ahijah the Shilonite."

Let's stop there for just a moment. There's an important principle in these verses. "The King did not listen to the people, for this turn of events was from the Lord." Did Rehoboam choose to answer this way? Certainly! Was Rehoboam responsible for the brutal way he responded? Absolutely! Was God behind the scenes ensuring that His prophetic Word to Jeroboam would be fulfilled? Yes. Very often in Scripture we find human mistakes playing into the overall plan of God. We must not excuse those mistakes just because God uses them for

His purposes, but at the same time, we must not panic when we see those mistakes because we can be sure that God is ultimately in control, working out all things after the counsel of His own Will.

Now the result of Rehoboam's decision to reject the advice the elders gave was the permanent dissolution of the United Monarchy: "When all Israel saw that the King refused to listen to them, they answered the King: "What share do we have in David, what part in Jesse's son? To your tents, O Israel! Look after your own House, O David!"

King Rehoboam barely manages to escape from Shechem back to Jerusalem. Then the Northern ten tribes call Jeroboam and make him their king, with only the tribes of Judah and Benjamin remaining loyal to the House of David.

I want us to apply what we find here to our own hearts and lives

There is a reason why certain stories like this are included in the Scriptures. Obviously, volumes could have been written about the life of Rehoboam. Why is this particular story preserved? I suspect it is because God knows that refusing to listen to our elders is a common problem most of us struggle with at one point or another. So I would like to offer this application:

Following the advice of elders is one of the key protections God offers His people

Please understand that the term elders, as I am using it here, is not synonymous to an elected office in the church. My point is not to issue a defence of Elder power and authority in the church. Actually, if you do a word study on the term "elders" in the Bible you discover that it is used 188 times in the plural and six more times in the singular. It is very rarely used of an office but rather refers most often to an informal group of older men who, by virtue of their years and their experience, are viewed as having wisdom worth listening to.

Every city and town in ancient times had its group of elders, but they are clearly distinguished in many passages from other kinds of leaders, like judges, officials, and heads of tribes, nobles, and chiefs of families, princes, priests, and prophets. As best I can tell elders generally had no official authority, but they enjoyed strong moral authority. People knew who they were and ignored them only to their own detriment.

Perhaps Ezekiel 7: 26 gives us the greatest insight into the task of the elders. In this judgment passage we are told, "Calamity upon calamity will come, and rumour upon rumour. They will try to get a vision from the prophet; the teaching of the law by the priest will be lost, as will the counsel of the elders." Yes . . . In other words, vision comes from the prophet, teaching from the priest, and counsel from the elders.

With that information as background, I would suggest first that we should recognise the moral authority of our Elders.

First, Elders in the home.

I'm speaking of parents, of course. Parents are not automatically smarter than children, and "old" doesn't always mean "right". But God knows that parents are right most of the time, and He has decided that it is better for children to be the victims of an unwise decision by their parents once in a while than it is for every decision to be decided by a wrestling match between children and parents.

So God says to children in the home, "Children, obey your parents in the Lord, for this is right." I don't think that means "because the parents are always right," but rather "it is always right for children to respect and listen to their parents." The same Scripture text, Ephesians 6:1-3, goes on to say, "'Honour your father and mother' – which is the first commandment with a promise – 'that it may go well with you and that you may enjoy long life on the earth.'"

At the very least this verse offers a general promise, that – all other things being equal – an obedient child is going to be happier and is going to live longer than a disobedient one. That is just the opposite the way a disobedient child thinks. He thinks his disobedience is going to make him happier and gain him an advantage. Not so.

Second, Elders in society.

I believe the Scriptures make the assumption that the elders in society be respected and listened to. Again and again when Moses had something important to decide, he would bring together all the elders of Israel. He used them as sounding boards and as counsellors. He took them with him when he had important tasks to perform. The elders were also very involved in the application of the Mosaic Law to the lives of the people – kind of like informal judges so the courts weren't overwhelmed by the caseload.

Jeremiah laments the tragedy that has come upon Judah at the time of the Babylonian captivity with these words: "Princes have been hung up by their hands, elders are shown no respect. Young men toil at the millstones; Boys stagger under loads of wood. The elders are gone from the city gate." Clearly the prophet sees the absence of the elders as a sad day for the nation. I, for one, feel that our country is better off when we have older leaders in office. It's not that younger people have nothing to offer. Their enthusiasm and vision can be a great balance, but there is something about having seasoned veterans in key positions that helps me sleep a little better at night.

I wrote earlier that the term "elders" is not limited to an office; but neither should the office of elder be excluded from this discussion. The Apostle Paul writes in 1 Timothy 5:17, "The elders who direct the affairs of the church well are worthy of double honour." Of course, to be worthy of double honour they must also be worthy servants.

In 1 Peter 5:1-4 the expectations are spelled out pretty clearly: "To the elders among you, I appeal as a fellow elder, a witness of Christ's sufferings and one who also will share in the glory to be revealed: Be shepherds of God's flock that is under your care, serving as overseers – not because you must, but because you are willing, as God wants you to be; not greedy for money, but eager to serve; not lording it over those entrusted to you, but being examples to the flock."

Every once in a while I hear someone complain about the Church Eldership as though it were a faceless group of authority figures who sit off by themselves and render decisions in a vacuum that everyone else then has to live with. That's really not how it is in most places I know. These are a loving, caring group of godly men who pray earnestly for the congregation, who seek God's face constantly, and who make decisions with fear and trembling. I believe they are approachable, reasonable, and humble – not perfect, however. When they have made mistakes they have to acknowledge that to individuals and to the congregation. But I urge congregations to recognise that following the advice of Elders is one of the key protections God offers His people.

Let me ask you this: "Do you specifically make time to seek God's wisdom and wait for His reply concerning whatever crisis you may be facing? Where do you go when you need advice? Do you go to people who will tell you what you want to hear? Or do you seek advice from those experienced in the knowledge of God and His Word, who will tell you the truth?"

So far we have examined a key symptom of spiritual illness in Rehoboam's life: He rejected the advice the elders gave. But why did this happen? What was the root problem that caused this man who inherited the most powerful kingdom of his day to crash and burn? Rehoboam did evil because he had not set his heart on seeking the Lord. When we consult the account in 2 Chronicles 11 we learn some additional facts about Rehoboam.

First we learn that Rehoboam started off fairly well

Aside from that initial foolish decision to raise taxes and treat the people harshly and the resultant loss of over 80% of his Kingdom, Rehoboam actually had a fairly good beginning to his reign. He built up the towns, fortified the cities, and strengthened their defences. Even more importantly, when Jeroboam became King of the Northern tribes, many of the godly people abandoned the north and headed to Judah.

"The priests and Levites from all their districts throughout Israel sided with Rehoboam. The Levites even abandoned their pasturelands and property, and came to Judah and Jerusalem because Jeroboam and his sons had rejected them as priests of the LORD. And he appointed his own priests for the high places and for the goat and calf idols he had made. Those from every tribe of Israel who set their hearts on seeking the LORD, the God of Israel, followed the Levites to Jerusalem to offer sacrifices to the LORD, the God of their fathers. They strengthened the Kingdom of Judah and supported Rehoboam son of Solomon three years, walking in the ways of David and Solomon during this time."

That's really encouraging! Not only priests but also lay people were willing to give up their land and all their possessions to support Rehoboam.

There may come a time when God will call us to put our money where our mouth is, to forsake position and possessions to strengthen a minority who are faithful to God. We can be sure of one thing – when we seek first God's Kingdom and His righteousness, God has ways of adding to us all we need – and not just for three years but for good! Unfortunately, Rehoboam did not follow through on his good beginning. He made the same mistakes his father made.

First and foremost was his casual attitude toward the institution of marriage. Eventually, he acquired 18 wives and 60 concubines in all. That's not in the same league as his father Solomon, but clearly he was heading in the same dangerous direction.

Furthermore, in the last verse of the chapter we learn that he took many wives for his sons. He replaced the gold shields with bronze ones, pretending that nothing had changed. You can read a very interesting account in 2 Chronicles 12: "After Rehoboam's position as King was established and he had become strong, he and all Israel with him abandoned the law of the LORD. Because they had been unfaithful to the LORD, Shishak King of Egypt attacked Jerusalem in the fifth year of King Rehoboam. With twelve hundred chariots and sixty thousand horsemen and the innumerable troops of Libyans, Sukkites and Cushites that came with him from Egypt, he captured the fortified cities of Judah and came as far as Jerusalem. Then the prophet Shemaiah came to Rehoboam and to the leaders of Judah who had assembled in Jerusalem for fear of Shishak, and he said to them, "This is what the LORD says, 'You have abandoned me; therefore, I now abandon you to Shishak.'"

When the Lord says, "I will abandon you," you're in trouble. Fortunately He only says that to those who have already abandoned Him. Rehoboam and his leaders recognize the dangerous situation they are in, so they humble themselves before the Lord. And when the Lord sees that, He informs the prophet that He will not allow Shishak to destroy Jerusalem, but He will allow the Israelites to become subjects of the Egyptian monarch for a very specific purpose: "so that they may learn the difference between serving me and serving the kings of other lands."

Archaeologists have verified the key points of this account. In Karnak in Egypt they found a temple which records the campaign of this powerful Pharaoh and a list of the cities he destroyed in Judah – 150 of them. He came right up to the gates of Jerusalem and it was only by allowing him to clean out the treasury that Rehoboam was able to survive. He took everything, including the gold shields Solomon had made. So King Rehoboam made bronze shields to replace them and assigned these to the commanders of the guard on duty at the entrance to the royal palace.

"Whenever the King went to the Lord's temple, the guards went with him, bearing the shields, and afterward they returned them to the guardroom." Remember the incredible gold furnishings that were in the Temple. Among them were 500 golden shields which Solomon had made. They were intended to be symbols of the glory of God and His protection over His people. Shishak took them back to Egypt. But the most interesting part of the story is that Rehoboam apparently tried to cover up this disastrous loss so that the common people would not realize how devastating his defeat really was. So he fabricated bronze shields to look like gold shields. On state occasions they were brought out and used in the royal parade when he went up to the Temple to worship. Then they were taken back and hidden in the guards' rooms.

Solomon had displayed his shields openly in his house and in the Lord's House. Rehoboam hid these shields in the guardhouse. Do you know why? Because bronze tarnishes. They would start to turn green, and anyone who would look at them would think, "What has happened to the gold shields?" Then the cat would be out of the bag and they would realize that Rehoboam had sold out, and that the glory of Israel was gone.

Immediately following this account, the author of 2 Chronicles damns Rehoboam with faint praise: "Because Rehoboam humbled himself, the Lord's anger turned from him, and he was not totally destroyed. Indeed, there was some good in Judah." That's really sad when all God can say is that there was some good among His chosen people. They weren't totally corrupt, so they would not be totally destroyed. Then just a few verses later King Rehoboam's life is summed up: "He did evil because he had not set his heart on seeking the Lord." What does that mean? At the very least it means he had other priorities. The affairs of state took precedence over spiritual pursuits. You never find Rehoboam praying, and very rarely consulting the Lord through the prophets. He was obsessed with political alliances and protecting his northern flank from Jeroboam.

What has this got to say to us?

Anytime we fail to set our hearts on seeking the Lord, we are well on our way to spiritual failure. I want to try to apply this truth to our hearts by responding to each of the points we made a few moments ago about Rehoboam.

We observed first that he started off fairly well.

God is not impressed with good beginnings. There are many in Scripture who started off well but did not end well. The spiritual life is for the long haul. That's why the true heroes of the Bible are people like Abraham, Caleb, Deborah, David, John Mark, Priscilla, and Paul. None of them ran the race perfectly. In fact, nearly all of them committed grievous sins. But they didn't quit; they didn't allow their failures to be final. They pressed on to the end. In contrast, there were also many who started out in a blaze of glory but crashed and burned when the going got tough. An example is Demas, of whom Paul wrote, "Demas, because he loved this world, has deserted me and has gone to Thessalonica." We need to pay attention to

Psalm 119:112: “My heart is set on keeping your decrees to the very end.”

The second point made about Rehoboam is that he made the same mistakes his father made.

This is important. Our children will rarely surpass us spiritually. That's a scary thought, but there's a lot of evidence for it. There's something in First and Second Kings and Chronicles that stands out like a sore thumb. It's called the Second Generation Syndrome. With rare exception, children seem to minimise the spiritual commitment of their parents and maximise their mistakes. That puts a tremendous responsibility on us as parents to live authentic Christian lives in the home. Nothing destroys the faith of a child faster or more thoroughly than seeing a huge gap between what a parent professes and what he or she practices. It is incumbent upon us to make sure we pass on a living faith, not just a set of doctrines.

The third point made was that he replaced the gold shields with bronze ones, pretending nothing had changed.

The glory always fades when we live inauthentic lives, fake lives. What happens when for some reason or other we turn our back on the Lord and that relationship is marred? Well, he doesn't leave but the glory begins to fade. We begin to feel ourselves becoming irritable and irresponsible and hard to live with. We start yelling at the children and at our spouses, and we get anxious and troubled and worried and negative and frustrated. We rub people the wrong way. It occurs to us that we ought not to be that way, and we certainly don't want to give that impression. So we fabricate the righteousness of God. We make a cheap imitation. We try by self-effort to be patient and kind and loving. We drag out our bronze shields. But do you know what happens to bronze shields? They tarnish and corrode. We can't sustain by self-effort the righteousness of God.

Is there any sense in which you are faking it today? Attending church services, mouthing the right words, but you know in your heart you're just going through the motions. There's no time like right now to be honest with yourself and with God. Come clean with Him; tell Him you've had enough of just going through religious rites and rituals; ask the Holy Spirit to come in and spring-clean. End well, pass on the faith to your children, live authentic lives. Those are truths God wants us to learn from the sad life of Rehoboam, King of Judah.

One last thought. How differently would the life of both Rehoboam and the whole nation of Israel have turned out if there were just a couple of words changed in his epitaphs. If it said, "He listened to the advice the elders gave," and "He did right because he set his heart on seeking the Lord." What will your epitaph read?
Let's make sure it reads something like this . . . "Well done my good and faithful servant."

Chapter 4
Jeroboam
God Has The Last Word

The Bible tells us that biographies recorded in First and Second Kings aren't just ancient history. There are key lessons we can learn so that we can 'Reign In Life'. I have written about Solomon and Rehoboam. Now we come to 1 Kings 13 and King Jeroboam. Once again there's more here than an old story. Chapter 13 comes down to this: 'God Has The Last Word.' Another way of putting the same truth is that obedience to God's Word is essential for spiritual victory.

Let me set the historical stage

The United Monarchy of Israel, after a little over a century under the rule of Saul, David, and Solomon, endures a bloodless civil war and is split into two nations. Jeroboam is chosen as the new King of Israel that is the northern ten tribes, while Rehoboam, the son of Solomon, is left with only the tribes of Judah and Benjamin, including the capital city of Jerusalem. You thought trouble in the Holy Land was recent, but it's been going on for 3000 years! Jeroboam is worried that if he allows his people to go to Jerusalem to worship, they might waver in their loyalty and might once again give their allegiance to Rehoboam, so he decides to establish worship centres in two cities in the north – Dan and Bethel. This is not equivalent to planting two new churches in order to expand worship opportunities for the people. This is a direct violation of the commandment of God for all Israelites to go to Solomon's temple three times a year to meet with God and receive atonement for their sins. Instead Jeroboam sets up two golden calves in the cities of Dan and Bethel, and calls upon his people to worship them. In fact, he leads them in this false worship, appointing anyone who volunteered to be a priest.

Please give attention to a selection of verses from 1 Kings 13: "By the Word of the LORD a man of God came from Judah to Bethel, as Jeroboam was standing by the altar to make an offering. He cried out against the altar by the Word of the LORD . . . When King Jeroboam heard what the man of God cried out against the altar at Bethel, he stretched out his hand from the altar and said, "Seize him!" But the hand he stretched out toward the man shrivelled up, so that he could not pull it back. Also, the altar was split apart and its ashes poured out according to the sign given by the man of God by the Word of the LORD. Then the King said to the man of God, "Intercede with the LORD your God and pray for me that my hand may be restored." So the man of God interceded with the LORD, and the King's hand was restored and became as it was before. The king said to the man of God, "Come home with me and have something to eat, and I will give you a gift." But the man of God answered the King, "Even if you were to give me half your possessions, I would not go with you, nor would I eat bread or drink water here. For I was commanded by the Word of the LORD: 'You must not eat bread or drink water or return by the way you came.'" So he took another road and did not return by the way he had come to Bethel."

The account goes on to explain how a certain old prophet heard about this, met the prophet and asked him to go home with him and eat. "The man of God said, "I cannot turn back and go with you, nor can I eat bread or drink water with you in this place. I have been told by the Word of the LORD: 'You must not eat bread or drink water there or return by the way you came.'" The old prophet answered, "I too am a prophet, as you are. And an angel said to me by the Word of the LORD: 'Bring him back with you to your house so that he may eat bread and drink water.'" (But he was lying to him.) So the man of God returned with him and ate and drank in his house." Then the old prophet told his guest he had done the wrong thing and would die for it. Going on his way he was killed by a lion. "The older prophet went and buried him. Then: "he said to his sons, "When I die, bury me in the grave where the man of God is buried; lay my bones beside his bones. For the message he declared by the Word of the LORD against the altar in Bethel and against all the shrines on the high places in the towns of Samaria will certainly come true." "Even after this, Jeroboam did not change his evil ways." This is a strange story indeed. In fact, it is one of those parts of

Scripture that is often passed over in embarrassed silence. But remember, "all Scripture is God-breathed and is profitable . . . " (2 Timothy 3:16)

There are obviously some things about this story that scream out at us, "Lord, that's not fair!" Twice this true man of God from Judah has rebuffed efforts to distract him from single-minded obedience to God's revealed will. Clearly he could have received a handsome honorarium from the King had he agreed to go home with him, but he refuses. He even refuses the offer of an older, more experienced prophet, which also must have taken a good bit of courage. Why is he subjected to still a third temptation, one so convincing that almost anyone would be tempted to fall for it? And why does he have to lose his life for such a seemingly trivial mistake? These are natural questions that arise in our minds. But what we must come to grips with above all else is that disobedience to a clear Word from God is never a trivial mistake. It is not our job to weigh the commands of God and decide which ones are important and which ones are optional. None are optional.

When God has spoken, absolutely nothing supersedes it. Now this is true both of God's predictions and of His commandments. Our focus is going to be on His commands, but I don't want to overlook the prediction that precipitated this whole incident.

What He prophesies will come to pass. The man of God from Judah cries out against Jeroboam's idolatrous altar and predicts two things by the Word of the Lord. That phrase, "by the Word of the Lord," is a technical phrase that identifies his message as clearly coming from God. This was not guesswork on the part of the man of God; it is not a strong impression; it is the Word of the Lord. The first prediction he makes is that a person named Josiah would be born to the House of David and this king would sacrifice the very priests who were making sacrifices on Jeroboam's altar.

That prediction came to pass exactly as the man of God prophesied, but not until 300 years later! For the fascinating fulfilment of the very details of this prophecy, including the sacrifice of these very priests, occurred 300 years after his death.

The second prediction of the man of God from Judah is given as an immediate sign that the first prediction would eventually come to pass. He said, "The altar will be split apart and the ashes on it will be poured out." And that's exactly what happens while Jeroboam is standing there with his shrivelled and paralysed hand. Sometimes what God predicts happens immediately; sometimes what God predicts takes a long time to happen; but whether long-term or short-term, God's Word is always fulfilled. You can count on it.

What He commands must be obeyed. The Lord had told the man of God from Judah not to eat or drink or return by the way he came. The will of God in this matter was perfectly clear to him, for twice he himself spells it out. Is God's will always as clear to us? No, not if you're talking about which direction to go home from work. But on most important issues it is. Should we lie, steal, cheat, get drunk, commit adultery, or covet? No. Should we treat others with respect and love and the same kind of care and concern we want to be treated with? Yes. There can be no doubt that God has spoken on these matters, and He has spoken clearly.

But let's bring this a little closer to home for those of us who consider ourselves to have high moral standards and to be kind-hearted toward others. Here are five truths that Rick Warren says we would agree with, at least intellectually:

You were planned for God's pleasure (worship).

You were formed for God's family (fellowship).

You were created to become like Christ (discipleship).

You were shaped for serving God (ministry).

You were made for mission (evangelism).

But in all honesty, how many of us creatively disobey the "commands" to worship, fellowship, spend time in the Bible and in prayer, serve one another, and share our faith? We get so caught up in ourselves so we don't have time for these commandments of God. We rationalise our spiritual apathy and suffer greatly because of it.

There are many rationalisations besides busyness we use to disobey what God tells us. Several of those factors are found in this story and I want to address them individually.

No relationship justifies disobedience

Did you notice what the old prophet said to the man of God after he first refused to come home with him? "I too am a prophet, as you are. Hey, we're equals. We're both ordained. In fact, I've been ordained a lot longer than you. Do you think I would ask you to do something if it weren't okay with God?" But, ministerial credentials are no guarantee that a person is speaking for God. Some clergy are just blind guides of the blind.

If you look back at verse 11, you discover that this old prophet was living in Bethel. We discover in 2 Chronicles 11 that when the northern tribes split from the south and Jeroboam was chosen as King, all the priests and Levites and godly people abandoned their positions and possessions and fled south to support Rehoboam. Why then is this old prophet still in Bethel, a centre of idolatry in the Northern Kingdom? The best reason I can come up with is that this old prophet has sold out to Jeroboam. He is an apostate prophet.

Every once in a while I meet an older minister, say in his 60's (I know that's really old, but occasionally a preacher does reach that advanced stage), who is part of a denomination that no longer holds to biblical authority and whose leaders are not even embarrassed by the radical heresy that is regularly taught in college and many of their pulpits. But the old minister I'm talking about still seems to believe the Gospel and personally embraces the truths of the Christian faith. In the course of the conversation I will ask him, "Tell me, why do you stay in a denomination with which you have virtually nothing in common?" And I get an answer something like this: "Well, I'm just a few years from getting my pension, so I just try to isolate myself from the denomination. I don't bother them, and most of the time they don't bother me."

There may be good reasons for staying in an apostate denomination (like being a missionary in the darkness), but getting one's pension is not one of them. I wonder if something like that wasn't the reason the old prophet had stayed in Bethel. Perhaps he was already getting a pension from the King and wasn't willing to leave his position and his possessions to go south like the godly priests and prophets did. In fact, he might even get a raise from the King if he could manage to deceive and destroy this young whippersnapper prophet who had embarrassed Jeroboam.

The point I think we need to learn from the claim of the old prophet ("I too am a prophet, as you are,") is that relationship should never be allowed to trump the Word of God. And don't think that doesn't happen in the church today! The Bible makes it crystal clear that a believer should not marry an unbeliever. Yet I often hear people saying, "But what if I really love him and he treats me well?" Or, "What if she's showing some interest in spiritual things? I'm just sure she'll eventually become a Christian." Or, "I know a case where a friend of mine married an unbeliever and the person became a believer, and now they attend church together." The fact remains, God's Word says a believer should not marry an unbeliever, and no relationship trumps the Word of God.

No claims of authority justify disobedience

Look at the next thing the old prophet says to the man of God from Judah: "I too am a prophet, as you are. And an angel said to me by the Word of the Lord: 'Bring him back with you to your house so that he may eat bread and drink water.'" Wow! How can you argue with that? Not only does he claim to have heard from an angel, but the angel also supposedly spoke "by the Word of the Lord."

This is the argument that finally breaks down the defences of the man of God and leads him into disobedience. And this is the kind of argument that is causing so many in our day to follow false teachers into all kinds of heresy. But the

Apostle Paul warned us in Galatians 1, "Even if we or an angel from Heaven should preach a gospel other than the one we preached to you, let him be eternally condemned!" Now clearly Paul's point is hypothetical because no angel from Heaven would ever preach another Gospel, but even if he did, he has no authority to change what God has established. The fact is that an angel did not speak to the old prophet – he was lying about it, as the story makes clear; so the man of God had no business relying on a second-hand report about a revelation from some angel, when God had made His will directly known to him in the first place.

There are all kinds of claims to religious authority being made today. Every cult on the face of the earth is the result of someone claiming to have heard some new revelation from God . . . truth that directly contradicts what God has already spoken. Even within the Christian church we have many today who are claiming, "The Lord told me this" and "The Lord told me that."

I caught a few minutes of a bizarre sermon from a popular radio preacher who was having his congregation of thousands chant, "I will never be poor another day in my life," supposedly on the basis of a revelation he had received. There is an authority crisis in the church today, and that authority crisis is directly related to an abandonment of our one true and reliable authority – the Word of God.

We can speak to the sins of the church without being prideful; in fact, we must. I have been in churches which have gone through some painful experiences of discipline, and each time you hear from a few, “You’re not being gracious!” or “Why not just forgive and forget?” or “He who is without sin should cast the first stone.” But I’d rather have a few people think we’ve been ungracious, than to disobey God’s commands and end up bringing disrepute on the Name of Christ. That doesn’t mean we are willing to sacrifice individuals for the sake of the organisation. We believe in restoration, and we practice it when possible, but not at the expense of truth or at the expense of other potential victims.

There is another factor that is often used to justify disobedience to God. And I’m lumping several related issues together:

No reason, intuition or emotions justify disobedience.

Our society is split on whether reason is king (that’s modernism) or intuition and emotions are king (that’s more post-modern). Most of our culture would choose one or the other, either “I must do what reason tells me is right” or “I must do what my heart tells me is right.” But the fact is, neither one should be allowed to supersede a clear word from the Lord.

Consider 1 Kings 20. We're skipping over quite a few years and several Kings, but the brief story here is so relevant to our text that I think we should consider these two accounts together. Ahab is now King of Israel and is being threatened by his northern neighbour Syria or Aram. Their King, Ben-Hadad (well known in ancient history for his part in the great battle of Karkar), is threatening the nation of Israel with a large and powerful army. In his initial encounter with Ben-Hadad, Ahab obeys God, and God gives him a significant victory. He then obeys God a second time and God gives him another victory. In fact, he actually captures the Syrian King and takes him hostage. But then Ahab disobeys. Despite God's Order to execute Ben-Hadad, Ahab decides to negotiate a deal instead. In exchange for land concessions and trade concessions, he agrees to let Ben-Hadad go. Now pay attention to the unique means God uses to teach Ahab that his disobedience is inexcusable and fatal.

The end of verse 34 says: "So he (Ahab) made a treaty with him (Ben-Hadad), and let him go. By the Word of the LORD one of the sons of the prophets said to his companion (a fellow-prophet), "Strike me with your weapon," but the man refused. So the prophet said, "Because you have not obeyed the LORD, as soon as you leave me a lion will kill you." And after the man went away, a lion found him and killed him. The prophet found another man and said, "Strike me, please." So the man struck him and wounded him. Satisfied with his wound, this prophet covers his head with bandages (presumably with the blood oozing out) and waits alongside the road for Ahab to come by. The King stops his chariot when he sees this badly wounded man, and the prophet tells him this fictitious story: "I was in battle when a prisoner was placed in my charge. I was told that the penalty for letting him escape was my life or a talent of silver. Well, I got busy and all of a sudden the prisoner was gone. Do you think the judgment is fair?" And Ahab responds, "Sure it's fair. You agreed to it, didn't you?" Then the prophet removes his head bandage and Ahab recognises him as a prophet. He informs Ahab that the fictitious story is about him. He has let Ben-Hadad escape and God is going to make him pay with his life. (And, as a matter of history, Ahab is later killed in another battle with Ben-Hadad, which would never have happened if Ahab had done what God told him). But not only does Ahab lose his life for disobedience; so does this poor prophet who refuses to slug another prophet, just so the first prophet can act out an object lesson for King Ahab!

Again I think we must assume that prophets had a God-given capacity to discern the voice of the Lord. Once God's will was discerned there was nothing that should interfere with obedience, nothing whatever. But this prophet in Chapter 20 allows other considerations to interfere with his obedience. Perhaps he thought, "It's not reasonable to strike another person; besides he might hit me back and I can't afford any time off work." Or "Intuition tells me that God would never want me to do anything violent; surely He was joking." Or "This prophet is my friend, and I'm not going to treat a friend that way. My emotions won't allow me to do that." Normally speaking I would agree with all three of those statements. Under normal circumstances reason, intuition and emotions are all God-given controls that help us govern our behaviour and behave in a civil manner. But they cannot be allowed to trump a Word from the Lord.

To obey is better than going to church, to obey is better than prayer, to obey is better than witnessing. The point is not that you can only do one or the other, but rather that if you do any of those things without obedience, they are spiritually worthless.

So far, we have spent all our time demonstrating from these two Old Testament stories that when God has spoken, absolutely nothing supersedes it.

There is a second point which, though very brief, is just as clear in these accounts: When God's Word is clear, disobedience is taken seriously by God. The man of God from Judah lost his life due to his disobedience. The prophet in Chapter 20 lost his life for the same reason and by the same means.

I must tell you I'm very glad God doesn't deal with disobedience as abruptly and harshly today as he did in Jeroboam's day; my suspicion is that my radio audience would be very small. (But of course, there would be no one in the studio either, so it wouldn't matter). But the fact that God doesn't operate the same way does not mean He no longer considers disobedience serious. Just as much is said about the importance of obedience and the consequences of disobedience in the New Testament as in the Old Testament. And even today I see the sad consequences of sin in many people's lives, including my own; much of that is the Lord's discipline. I see broken lives, broken families, and all kinds of addictions, wasted potential. It would be very dangerous indeed for us to conclude that God doesn't care anymore when we violate His known will.

Now there is one more very important issue we must address: How do we know when God has spoken? There is no doubt in these two stories that the prophets who were killed by the lions knew what God had said. In the first account the prophet himself flatly says so. In the second story it says, "By the Word of the Lord one of the sons of the prophets said to his companion, "Strike me with your weapon." There's that phrase again, "by the Word of the Lord." He knew the message came from the Lord. So neither prophet could argue that he didn't know what God's will was. He could only try to rationalise his disobedience because of other considerations.

God doesn't speak in the same way today as He did then. Oh, some people claim He does, and that's why you hear a lot of them saying, "God told me x," or "God told me y." But I don't believe it. I see no evidence in the church today that God is speaking in the same manner He used with the Old Testament prophets. In fact, the Bible actually tells me I should not expect that.

Hebrews 1:1 says, "In the past God spoke to our forefathers through the prophets at many times and in various ways, but in these last days He has spoken to us by his Son." Jesus is the ultimate revelation. And how do we find the truth about Jesus? Only through the Bible, the written Word of God. I am tempted to say that through this book and only through this book can we know what God has spoken. But that's not quite accurate.

God speaks to individuals through His Holy Spirit. He gives them individual guidance and insight and direction. I have no doubt about that because the New Testament speaks frequently of a believer being "led" by the Spirit, and I have experienced it myself.

But there are certain caveats I would immediately attach to that statement.

First, the direction a believer receives that way is personal–i.e. direction for his own life, not direction for the whole church.

Second, God will never give personal direction that contradicts the written Word of God. When that radio preacher I listened to in my travels through the mid-west of America the other night was telling his congregation that God had told Him that it is a sin to be poor, I can state without any fear of contradiction that he was either lying or deluded, because God cannot contradict Himself, and the Bible makes it absolutely clear that one can be in great poverty and spiritually rich at the same time.

I also believe the Holy Spirit may speak through the spiritual leaders of a church to give direction to that church, but not for the universal church. The clearest way God speaks to us, individually and corporately, is through His Word.

God speaks to the Church through the Bible, the Word of God. This book is God's Book in the way that no other book in history is. This is the living and powerful Word of God. This Book contains all you need to know to live a godly life. This Book contains all the doctrines you need to know. God has spoken in this Book, and if God has spoken, it is our responsibility to obey. And not merely obey, but obey from the heart.

Let me ask you this question: Is there some clear teaching or truth from God's Word that you have ignored because of some relationship or some false claim to authority. Have you violated His revealed will on the basis of your own reason, or intuition, or emotions? If so, what will you do about it after reading this book?

I suggest a course of action

I urge you to cease immediately, to confess your disobedience, and to commit yourself today to follow God's revealed will no matter where it takes you. That's really not very risky, because God won't take you anywhere that is harmful.

In conclusion I want to draw your attention to one particular commandment of God which is always fatal if you disobey. And that is His command to repent of your sins and be obedient to the Gospel of Jesus Christ.

2 Thessalonians 1 says, " . . . when the Lord Jesus is revealed from Heaven in blazing fire with his powerful angels, He will punish those who do not know God and do not obey the Gospel of our Lord Jesus."

What does it mean to "obey" the Gospel? It means to repent of your sins and place your faith in the fact that Jesus died on the cross for your sins and to trust Him and Him alone for your eternal salvation. I call upon you today to obey the command of Scripture to "believe on the Lord Jesus Christ and you will be saved."

If you are already a believer in Jesus Christ, I warn you as well that God expects explicit obedience from His children – not tolerance of sin, not reasoned arguments, not religious excuses, but obedience.

Chapter 5
Asa
Help From The Wrong Source

Most of us are naturally inclined to turn to God when we are at the end of our rope and hopelessly inadequate to meet a particular challenge. But it's when we feel completely adequate and think we can do it on our own that we most need to rely on God. If that sounds strange to you, then you definitely need to consider the life of Asa, King of Judah. His experience demonstrates that our greatest failures often come at our points of greatest strength. Reliance on our own resources, our own skill, and our own adequacy can be fatal.

The epitaph I have chosen for this man comes from an incident very late in his life: "He did not seek help from the Lord, but only from the physicians." I acknowledge up front that if an epitaph's purpose is to accurately summarise a person's life, this one may not be entirely fair, for Asa was, for the most part, a godly king and a successful ruler. However, at two decisive points in his life he failed to trust in God, and the results were national and personal tragedy.

I'm actually going to write more on the positive aspects of Asa's life than on the negative, first because most of his life was indeed exemplary, and second because we need to recognize that there is danger in failing to trust the Lord even for those who are, for the most part, godly and spiritually successful. In other words, this chapter is not primarily for spiritual losers, though there is also something you can learn if you view yourself that way; rather it is for those who are successful spiritual leaders.

Let's begin by trying to put our text in historical perspective.

Asa's life is recorded for us in both 1 Kings and 2 Chronicles. We're going to focus on the account in 2 Chronicles. The United Monarchy of Israel was divided upon King Solomon's death in 931 BC, and his son Rehoboam succeeded him. Rehoboam followed his father in his mistakes but not in his wisdom, and his Kingdom was split into two parts. Jeroboam became the King of Israel, taking the northern ten tribes, while Rehoboam was left with just two tribes, called the Kingdom of Judah. Rehoboam reigned for seventeen years and was followed by his son Abijah, who had an unremarkable reign of three years. Abijah, in turn, was followed by his son Asa, who ruled in Jerusalem for 41 years.

That remarkable length of time is made even more astounding when we discover that his reign in Judah spanned that of the first 8 Kings of Israel.

There were two distinct periods in Asa's life. The first 35 years of his reign were peaceful and prosperous; the latter 6 years were quite the opposite. Why? The writer makes it abundantly clear: When Asa did what was good and right in the eyes of the Lord, he received the blessings of peace and prosperity. When Asa failed to trust in the Lord, he experienced defeat, disease, and death. That is the simple outline of his life there in 2 Chronicles 14, 15.

Frankly, it's hard to imagine how a ruler could be any better than this great-grandson of Solomon was for his first 35 years in office. 2 Chronicles 15:17 says, "Asa's heart was fully committed to the Lord all his life."

In 2 Chronicles 14: 2 we read: "Asa did what was good and right in the eyes of the LORD his God. He removed the foreign altars and the high places, smashed the sacred stones and cut down the Asherah poles. He commanded Judah to seek the LORD, the God of their fathers, and to obey His laws and commands. He removed the high places and incense altars in every town in Judah, and the Kingdom was at peace under him. He built up the fortified cities of Judah, since the land was at peace. No one was at war with him during those years, for the LORD gave him rest. "Let us build up these towns," he said to Judah, "and put walls around them, with towers, gates and bars. The land is still ours, because we have sought the LORD our God; we sought Him and he has given us rest on every side." So they built and prospered."

The first thing we discover here is that Asa removed the pagan altars, idols, and high places.

Some of this pagan stuff was left over from Solomon, who built temples for his foreign wives, but it's amazing how widespread it had become among the common people in Judah. "Leaders set the standard," you know. Solomon should have known he couldn't admit idolatry into the royal house without it impacting the rest of the country.

I think we need to realize that Asa's actions here took a great deal of courage. People become very attached to false worship; in fact, they can become quite fanatical in defending their false views of God. But Asa didn't just hang a "closed" sign on the pagan shrines. He smashed the sacred stones and cut down the Asherah poles, which were both representations of these false deities. To put it in modern terms, he shut down the adult bookstores, ran the abortionists out of town, and legislated against the casinos. He cleaned up. Yet Asa was aware that it is never enough to remove evil, for something worse can take its place; evil must be replaced with good.

He commanded Judah to seek the Lord and to obey His laws and commands. He knew that obedience to the revealed will of God is the secret to spiritual victory.

Eleven different times in Asa's reign the term "seeking God" is used. The message is clear throughout: When God's people seek Him they find Him, because He is not hiding. And when they find Him, they experience His blessing and spiritual prosperity. But seeking God always involves obedience. One can't at the same time seek God and violate His commands.

He built up the defences of the country while there was peace. It's a curious thing that in the Old Testament God seemed to approve the strengthening of defences in times of peace, but He often rebuked the nation for doing the same thing in times of war. When threatened severely they were to rely on God; when not threatened they were to take wise precautions.

There may be a universal principle here: If we act wisely when times are good, we may not face so many bad times.

He enjoyed a miraculous victory over his enemies after calling on the Lord. In the last half of Chapter 14 we read about a major military threat against Asa in about the tenth year of his reign. We are told he had a strong army of 580,000 brave fighting men, equipped with shields, spears, and bows. However, coming against them was a vast army from Cush or Ethiopia, and this army was equipped with chariots, comparable to tanks in our day. Asa went out to meet this threat, and battle positions were set up not far south of Jerusalem.

And Asa prayed. "Then Asa called to the LORD his God and said, 'LORD, there is no one like you to help the powerless against the mighty. Help us, O LORD our God, for we rely on you, and in your Name we have come against this vast army. O LORD, you are our God; do not let man prevail against you.'" I love this prayer. It's short, it's direct, and it's effective:

First, he declares his confidence in the supremacy of God: "There is no one like You."

Second, he recognises his own inadequacy – he himself is the powerless against the mighty.

Third, he asks God to help and declares his total reliance on God.

It's possible, you know, to ask God to help but then not rely on Him. How many times have we prayed something like this, "Lord, I have no idea how to solve this problem. It's way beyond me. I need Your help. I've turning it over to you." Then as soon as we get up off our knees we say to ourselves, "Now what am I going to do about that problem?" Not Asa. He gave the problem to God and relied on Him to resolve it.

Asa is doing nothing other than what Solomon, his great-grandfather, called upon the people to do when he dedicated the Temple perhaps 65 years earlier. He prayed, "When your people go to war against their enemies, wherever you send them, and when they pray to you toward this city you have chosen and the Temple I have built for your Name, then hear from Heaven their prayer and their plea, and uphold their cause." And the result is that God gives Asa a great victory. The enemy suffers a terrible defeat and the men of Judah carry off a huge amount of plunder, returning triumphantly to Jerusalem. Though we aren't given any details about how He did it, it is made absolutely clear that the Lord won this great victory.

In 2 Chronicles 15, we see further reforms on the part of Asa, which pave the way for major revival. A prophet named Azariah comes to Asa after this victory over the Cushites. His message is one of hope and promise: "Listen to me, Asa and all Judah and Benjamin. The LORD is with you when you are with him. If you seek Him, He will be found by you, but if you forsake Him, He will forsake you. (Then the prophet goes back through history to show how God had always been there for them.) But as for you, be strong and do not give up, for your work will be rewarded." And indeed Asa does not give up but rather takes courage and renews his reformation efforts. He removes any leftover idols from the whole country, he repairs the altar of Solomon's temple, and then he calls all the people together for a solemn assembly. Large numbers come from all over the country of Judah, and even from the Northern Kingdom of Israel, too, when they see that the Lord is Asa's God. A great revival results, including sacrifices, worship, the making of covenants and oaths, and exuberant demonstrations through shouting and musical instruments. It is summarised this way: "They sought God eagerly, and He was found by them. So the Lord gave them rest on every side."

Then a very interesting thing is noted for us in verse 16: "Asa deposed his own grandmother due to her idolatry." That's significant. Generally kings were of the mind that laws were for other people and the king's family was exempt. Not so for Asa. No one was exempt from the expectation of whole-hearted loyalty to God. Since the Queen Mother had made a repulsive Asherah pole (not unlike a Totem Pole), he removed her, cut down her pole, broke it, and burned it in the Jerusalem dump. That must have had quite an impact on the country!

Leaders have to set the standards high for their own lives and for their families. The Apostle Paul recognises the importance of this when he gives qualifications for leaders in the church. He says, "If anyone does not know how to manage his own family, how can he take care of God's church?" This is not an unrealistic call of perfection on a leader's family; it is a call for leaders to put their responsibilities as spouses and parents ahead of their responsibilities as leaders so that they have the moral authority to lead. Asa was a good example in this regard. His heart was fully committed to the Lord all his life.

In verse 17 we read, "Although he did not remove the high places from Israel, Asa's heart was fully committed to the Lord all his life." Now if you are really alert, you may have noticed an apparent contradiction with 2 Chronicles 14:5, where we read, "He removed the high places and incense altars in every town in Judah." But it's actually not a contradiction, because 14:5 says he removed them from Judah, while 15:17 says he did not remove them from Israel. Asa was King of Judah and he did indeed remove the high places from his own country. What he did not do is to remove all the idolatry from the parts of the neighbouring country of Israel which his armies occupied. Perhaps he should have, but God doesn't hold him responsible for that.

But there's another confusing issue raised here, and that is how Asa can be said to be fully committed to the Lord all his life when we are going to discover in Chapter 16 that he failed to trust the Lord in two major areas during his last 6 years as King. I think the answer is that deep devotion to the Lord does not imply perfect behaviour. I'm glad for that reminder. It's easy to beat ourselves up and question whether we really love the Lord or are even truly converted after a miserable failure. Nor is it always wrong to ask such questions. But Asa's case convinces me that it is possible to experience spiritual failure while still being fully committed to the Lord.

The question is, "Where is our heart?" Do we feel deep sorrow when we do fail Him? Are we like David, who blamed no one but himself and humbled himself before the Lord? Do we run back to God and earnestly seek restoration?

The final thing I want to note is that Asa enjoyed peace until the thirty-fifth year of his reign.

Peace was one of the principal blessings God gave to Asa in response to his godly actions. Throughout the Old Testament "peace" is not only the absence of war but economic prosperity and social well-being as well. Imagine 35 consecutive years of peace and prosperity. Britain has never experienced that; few countries ever have. Asa and his nation of Judah did experience it because he did what was good and right in the eyes of the Lord.

But now we come to the latter part of Asa's reign; and here we discover a second fundamental truth: When Asa failed to trust in the Lord, he experienced defeat, disease, and death. Chapter 16 opens with these words: "In the thirty-sixth year of Asa's reign Baasha king of Israel went up against Judah and fortified Ramah to prevent anyone from leaving or entering the territory of Asa king of Judah." Israel and Judah were never very friendly to one another, but Baasha now decides to act very aggressively toward his southern neighbour. He fortifies Ramah, a town 6 miles north of Jerusalem, to cut off a major trade route from the east. We learn from 1 Kings 15:16 that there were skirmishes between Baasha and Asa throughout their reigns, but this is certainly the biggest threat yet.

Based upon his past experience and behaviour we might assume that Asa would go to the Lord and seek His help with this new threat. But Asa is no longer a young King; he is more secure now; he has a larger army; he certainly has had more diplomatic experience. So he decides to handle this threat by himself. Threatened by Baasha, King of Israel, he relied on political solutions instead of the Lord. He concocts a plan: He will take silver and gold out of the treasuries of the Lord's Temple, as well as out of his own house, to bribe Ben-Hadad (there's the same nemesis from Syria or Aram we saw last time). The plan is that Ben-Hadad will break his treaty with Baasha and begin to attack the northern cities of Israel. Then Baasha will have to abandon his threat against Judah in order to protect his northern flank.

There are two problems here

First, Asa is establishing a political alliance in lieu of dependence upon God. Second, he is calling upon a pagan nation to help him fight against his fellow-Israelites. Although Israel was in apostasy and was acting aggressively toward Judah, conspiring with foreign nations against them is outrageous. But it worked. In fact, it worked so well that Baasha abandoned Ramah entirely, allowing Asa's men to carry away from Ramah all the stones and timber Baasha had been using for his fortifications. With the materials Asa was able to build up two of his own cities.

Most people would be tempted to give Asa an 'A' for diplomacy and skill in removing a major threat. But God gave him an 'F'. In fact, God sent another prophet, this one named Hanani, to say to him: "Because you relied on the King of Aram and not on the LORD your God, the army of the King of Aram has escaped from your hand. Were not the Cushites and Libyans a mighty army with great numbers of chariots and horsemen? Yet when you relied on the LORD, he delivered them into your hand. For the eyes of the LORD range throughout the earth to strengthen those whose hearts are fully committed to Him. You have done a foolish thing, and from now on you will be at war."

Instead of congratulating the King for his clever victory, the prophet predicts judgment upon him for his foolish behaviour. He was foolish because he did not take into consideration the character of God, particularly His omniscience and omnipotence. God's omnipresence, represented by His eyes roving throughout the earth, enables Him to know those whose hearts are fully committed to Him, and His omnipotence strengthens them. This is not something God does on the weekends. It is not something He does just in church or holy places. It's not His hobby or after-hours recreation. This is what God is doing all the time everywhere. God's eyes are everywhere always, so that He never misses one single opportunity any time, anywhere to demonstrate His power on behalf of weak people who rely on Him and not man.

This is why Asa's unbelief was folly. King Asa reacts to the prophet's words in two ways, both bad. First, he throws the prophet in prison, and second, he brutally oppresses some of the people, presumably those who were sympathetic with the prophet. How tragic when we react to the discipline of the Lord with more sin! But how often do we do that? We get caught up in some wrong behaviour, we begin feeling guilty, so we stop coming to church and pull away from our Christian friends. We end up actually compounding the problem! Or we fail to give as we should and end up in financial trouble, and so we stop giving altogether. Or we have a fight at home with our spouse, and instead of asking for forgiveness, we go out and confide in someone else who takes our side and confirms us in our sinful attitudes. There's only one right way to deal with sin – that's repentance, confession, and acceptance of God's forgiveness.

There is a second event in which Asa failed to trust the Lord in his final years.

We read from 2 Chronicles 16:12, 13: "In the thirty-ninth year of his reign Asa was afflicted with a disease in his feet. Though his disease was severe, even in his illness he did not seek help from the LORD, but only from the physicians. Then in the forty-first year of his reign Asa died and rested with his fathers." Afflicted with a severe disease, he relied on his doctors instead of the Lord. There seems to me to be a parallel in these two stories. Asa believed he had sufficient resources in both cases to handle the problem by himself. With Baasha he had diplomatic resources. In regard to the disease in his feet he had medical resources. But the sin for which Asa is rebuked (be sure to catch this!) is not that he sought help from his doctors. It's that he sought help *only* from his doctors.

If we were to conclude from this passage of Scripture that it is wrong to consult with medical doctors, we would miss the whole point. There are people who draw such conclusions, but they cannot justify their views from this story, or, in my estimation, from any Scripture text rightly interpreted. The Scriptures show no hesitation about taking advantage of good medical care. But using ordinary means is never to be divorced from seeking divine assistance. The reason is simple: God can heal without doctors, but the doctors can heal only with God's help and permission.

I close this Chapter by answering a key question: What does it mean to "trust in the Lord," and when should we do it? Trusting in the Lord is relying on Him as the ultimate source of help for all of life. Proverbs 3:5, 6 is one of the best-known passages that challenges us to trust Him: "Trust in the LORD with all your heart and lean not on your own understanding; in all your ways acknowledge Him, and He will make your paths straight." The opposite of trusting in the Lord is leaning on your own understanding, your own resources, and your own ability. This verse answers the second part of our question as well, "when should we trust the Lord?" – "in all your ways", i.e. at all times. There is no time when it's not important to trust the Lord.

I return to where I started. It is natural, almost automatic, to turn to God when we reach the end of our rope. It's natural to lean on Him when we've been served papers by an angry spouse or when we discover one of our teenagers on drugs or when we are laid off from work. Unless we are really hardened toward God, we automatically turn to Him at a time like that. But what Asa teaches us is that it is crucial for us to turn to the Lord even when we think we have the resources to handle it ourselves.

Let's close by bringing together what we must learn from Asa

We must keep our contact line open with God. Many spiritual leaders seem oblivious to the battle that actually targets them. Perhaps they see the arsenal of weapons arrayed at them as benign. Fax machines, e-mail, telephones, beepers, an over-committed schedule, the press of people's needs, programme concerns, ministry agenda – these are the tools of mass destruction for spiritual leaders. Their development and deployment proceeds often without accountability. They threaten to shut down the spiritual leader's communion with God. Once that happens, the leader's effectiveness is destroyed. The leader becomes a casualty of a struggle that is as old as humanity – the drowning out of eternity by the screams of temporal concerns. "God-time" yields to "more pressing" concerns. The leader's communication line with the Commander begins to register static.

In response, the leader sometimes does exactly the wrong thing. Instead of repairing the communication by altering the busy schedule to make time for God, the leader compensates for the lack of divine guidance by increasing chat time with the established network. The only approval that satisfies, the "well-done" of the Commander-in-Chief, is set aside to curry favour from ministry constituents. Ministry efforts increase. So does the static. Episodic interruptions in the communication lines to God give way to a routine neglect. The leader goes off-line with Headquarters. Out of touch with Command, the leader begins to operate from the memory of previous Orders and Directives. Activity replaces productivity.

Genuine visionary enthusiasm and purpose give way to maintenance and routine, with an accompanying loss of joy and a rise in self-doubt.

Leaders who continue to act in this way become cut off from genuine divine intervention on their behalf. They begin to rely on their own diminishing reserves of spiritual firepower. They bank on their talents, their intellect, their relationship skills, and their position to cover their basic failure at the critical core function of their call. That function is to reflect God's heart to God's people. This cannot be done apart from a leader's firsthand knowledge of God's heart. This knowledge does not derive from historical encounters in a leader's past; it springs from a vibrant, up-to-date walk with the Almighty.

Devoid of a growing, personal, dynamic relationship with God, spiritual leaders become casualties. Some are removed from battle, too wounded to go on. Some remain engaged but are missing in action. Others desert God and His people. Perhaps the worst scenario is the tragic figure of a spiritual corpse going through ministry rituals like the zombies of science fiction horror movies. No amount of promise or talent or intelligence can ultimately shield the spiritual leader from some variation of this fate if contact with God is neglected.

Now, that's the bottom line. If contact or intimacy with God is neglected, no amount of promise or talent or intelligence or power or wealth or cleverness or experience can ultimately shield the spiritual leader from such a sad fate as Asa experienced.

Chapter 6
Ahab and Jezebel
Pay-Day Some-Day

The story is told about an airlines' gate agent. A crowded flight was cancelled. The agent was re-booking a long line of inconvenienced travellers. Suddenly an angry passenger pushed his way to the desk. He slapped his ticket down on the counter and said, "I HAVE to be on this flight and it has to be FIRST CLASS." The agent replied, "I'm sorry sir. I'll be happy to try to help you, but I've got to help these folks first, and I'm sure we'll be able to work something out." The passenger was unimpressed. He asked loudly, so that the passengers behind him could hear, "Do you have any idea who I am?" Without hesitating, the gate agent smiled and grabbed her public address microphone. "May I have your attention please?" she began, her voice bellowing throughout the terminal. "We have a passenger here at the gate WHO DOES NOT KNOW WHO HE IS. If anyone can help him find his identity, please come to Gate 17". The folks behind him in line began laughing hysterically. Although the flight was cancelled and people were late, they were no longer angry.

I grew up in a time when people spent a lot of time trying to "find themselves" (though I never quite figured out exactly what they were looking for). Do we have any idea who we are? Those of us who are Christians are royalty. That's what the New Testament says. 'A royal people'. And we are to 'reign in life' said Paul to Roman believers.

We don't always reign. Sometimes we are reigned over by people and circumstances. And that makes this book about the royal people of Old Testament days relevant. Our Bible makes it clear that these stories are not just names and dates from the past. They are examples through whom we can learn. So, we are exploring the royalty of 1 and 2 Kings. In this chapter we take a look at a King and Queen, Ahab and Jezebel. We will start with the incident with Naboth the Jezreelite, and I want you to read his story from 1 Kings 21.

This is a selection of verses

"There was an incident involving a vineyard belonging to Naboth the Jezreelite. The vineyard was in Jezreel, close to the palace of Ahab King of Israel. Ahab said to Naboth, "Let me have your vineyard to use for a vegetable garden, since it is close to my palace. In exchange I will give you a better vineyard or, if you prefer, I will pay you whatever it is worth." But Naboth replied, "The LORD forbid that I should give you the inheritance of my fathers." So Ahab went home, sullen and angry because Naboth the Jezreelite had said, "I will not give you the inheritance of my fathers." He lay on his bed sulking and refused to eat. His wife Jezebel came in and asked him, "Why are you so sullen? Why won't you eat?" He answered her, "Because I said to Naboth the Jezreelite, 'Sell me your vineyard; or if you prefer, I will give you another vineyard in its place.' But he said, 'I will not give you my vineyard.'" Jezebel his wife said, "Is this how you act as King over Israel? Get up and eat! Cheer up. I'll get you the vineyard of Naboth the Jezreelite."

She got trumped up charges going against Naboth and he was stoned to death. Jezebel then told her husband to take possession of the vineyard.

"When Ahab heard that Naboth was dead, he got up and went down to take possession of Naboth's vineyard."

God has said, "Vengeance is mine; I will repay." What He doesn't say is when. Those of us who believe in the wrath of God – and I regret to say that it appears we may be a slowly vanishing tribe – still have frequent struggles with the timing of God's justice. We sometimes get impatient with Heaven's Department of Justice, because wrongs often go un-remedied for a long time. But let's be sure we understand that it cuts both ways – while we are troubled that God doesn't judge the wicked in a timely manner, we should be grateful that He doesn't judge us that way.

In fact, I would say we all have plenty of reason to be thankful that God is, as the Scriptures often say, "Slow to anger." Slow, but not tardy. In fact, what appears to us as slowness is actually patience. That's what 2 Peter 3:9 tells us: "The Lord is not slow in keeping His promise, as some understand slowness. He is patient with you, not wanting anyone to perish, but everyone to come to repentance." Yet the very next verse says, "But the day of the Lord will come like a thief. The heavens will disappear with a roar; the elements will be destroyed by fire, and the earth and everything in it will be laid bare." God will avenge the blood of the righteous, and He will judge the wicked severely.

There is no event in Scripture which speaks more profoundly of the inevitable course of God's judgment than the story of Naboth that we have just read. The historical context is late in the reign of Ahab, King of Israel – about 850 BC. Ahab is married to Jezebel, a ruthless idol-worshiper who is clearly the power behind the throne. The prophet who is prominent in this story is Elijah the Tishbite – the same prophet who earlier defeated the 850 prophets of Baal and Asherah, but who then experienced a devastating slide into fear and depression.

This story is a key part of the comeback trail for Elijah

The first scene in our story has to do with a real estate venture: Ahab fails in his attempt to acquire Naboth's vineyard. Ahab had a summer palace in the town of Jezreel. Samaria was the capital of Israel, but Ahab preferred Jezreel because it was near the Mediterranean and had a nicer climate. On a certain day Ahab was admiring the lush and beautiful grounds of his palace when his eyes lighted upon a neighbouring vineyard which belonged to Naboth. And Ahab coveted this vineyard for a vegetable garden.

It's difficult to read about Ahab's covetousness without one's mind going back several centuries to the time when another King of Israel was walking on the roof of his palace in Jerusalem and his eyes lighted upon something that belonged to his neighbour, Uriah the Hittite, namely Uriah's wife, Bathsheba. He coveted, he stole, he murdered, and then he lied. And the Word of the Lord came to him through the prophet Nathan, saying, "I anointed you King over Israel and I delivered you from the hand of Saul. I gave your master's house to you, and your master's wives into your arms. I gave you the House of Israel and Judah. And if all this had been too little, I would have given you even more." David had so much, yet covetousness drove him to seize that which was not his.

Ahab undoubtedly owned countless acres of tillable soil, but covetousness drove him to seek one little piece of land more. It reminds us of the famous tycoon who was asked, "How much is enough?" His answer: "Just a little more."

We can say this much for Ahab, however. He had no intention of stealing Naboth's vineyard. He offered to pay a fair price or, if Naboth preferred, give him a better vineyard in its place. Looking at it from Naboth's viewpoint, there was much to commend this deal. He could demand a premium price and probably get it. Or he could receive an even better vineyard. And it was an opportunity to curry royal favour for himself and his family. Who wouldn't take a deal like this? From a purely human standpoint, there was everything to gain and almost nothing to lose. But Naboth refused. And he refused, not because of any ill will toward the king, nor to hold out for a better price, but rather because of his faithfulness to the Lord God and to his family.

According to the Law of Moses, Palestine was God's land and the Jewish people were His tenants. When the Israelites first conquered the Promised Land, God divided the land among the 12 tribes, and then further subdivided it by clans and families so that every family in Israel had a plot of ground they could call their own. This was unique in the ancient Near East. In most countries the kings and nobles owned the land and the common people worked it. But in Israel everyone owned a piece of land. Among the regulations in the Law of Moses that were designed to prevent property from being concentrated in the hands of a few rich and powerful people was one found in Leviticus 25:23: "The land must not be sold permanently, because the land is mine and you are but aliens and my tenants." The land could be leased for a period, but it was not to be sold permanently. If a family became destitute and found it necessary to sell their land, its ownership automatically reverted to them in the year of Jubilee, every fiftieth year.

Naboth was not destitute, nor did he have any reason to believe that wicked King Ahab would honour the Jubilee regulation, and so because of his faith in God, because of his desire to be obedient to God's commands, and in part, because of the precious memories of his family that were tied to that land, he turned down Ahab's offer.

In this I see a noble example of a husband and father who put the godly before the expedient, the eternal ahead of the temporal. Unfortunately, when one chooses to do the right thing, the results are not always ideal from the human standpoint. Sometimes tragedy happens, but a godly person chooses right anyway and trusts that a sovereign God will also do what is right.

What did Ahab do about Naboth's refusal? He pouted. Nor was this the first time, for Ahab was a man controlled by his passions and emotions. There he is, the King, whining like a whipped dog pouting like a spoiled child that has been denied one trinket in the midst of a thousand toys. There's the Commander in Chief of an army, made captive by Corporal Pity, made prisoner by Private Pout. Look at this old whale wallow and spout because he's denied minnow food. Listen to this old bear growl because he's denied a few drops of honey. Listen to this old crow shriek because he's denied the crumbs from one loaf of bread. Listen to this old lion roar because he's denied the cheese in a mousetrap. Listen to this old bull bellow for a bit of grass outside his own vast pastureland.

Yes, and get the duplicate of that portrait in thousands of people in our world today: who have diamond and ruby ability who are worth no more to Christ or to his church than a £12 note; people with pipe-organ abilities making no more music for Christ than a paper and comb; people with Formula car engine power doing bicycle work; with big-digger abilities doing teaspoon work; with incandescent light power making flickering candlelight for the cause of Christ.

Well, Ahab has failed in his real estate venture, but all hope is not lost so long as his wife Jezebel is by his side. In the second scene we see that Jezebel succeeds where Ahab failed. When she first appears here in Chapter 21, it is with solicitous concern for her husband Ahab. But that concern soon turns to sarcastic ridicule.

Jezebel very kindly inquires of her husband as to why he is feeling down and not eating. But when she learns that it is because Naboth has refused to sell his vineyard, she lashes out at him: "Are you King or aren't you? Do you have absolute authority or don't you? Are you going to allow that worthless peasant to thwart your desire? Arise, eat and let your heart be joyful. I will get you the vineyard of Naboth the Jezreelite." And this is no idle promise coming from the lips of Jezebel. Getting Naboth's vineyard would be a piece of cake for one as evil and unprincipled as she, for one who has no regard for the God of Israel or for righteousness, for one whose greatest concern in life is the satisfaction of her own lusts. And so we come to Jezebel's sinister plot against Naboth.

She writes letters on Ahab's stationery and uses his signet ring to seal them. In those letters she orders the local authorities in Jezreel to proclaim a fast, to set Naboth in the prisoner's dock, and to hire two worthless men to commit perjury, accusing him of high treason against the King and blasphemy against God. Sadly, the elders of Jezreel do exactly as Jezebel tells them to. They are so tyrannised by Jezebel and so afraid for their own lives that they lack the intestinal fortitude to stand up for the rights of this innocent family.

One cannot help but empathise with the tortured hearts of Naboth and his family as they face this sudden turn of events. Surely, Naboth protests his innocence to this kangaroo court. Surely, his wife and sons beg for mercy from the elders of the city. Surely, his wife screams out in anguish as her husband is stoned to death before her eyes and her sons are taken from her grasp and murdered along with their father to make sure they are not able to sue for return of the land at some time in the future.

And what is Ahab doing while this heinous deed is being perpetrated and Naboth's blood is seeping into the soil?

As soon as Jezebel receives word of Naboth's death she goes to Ahab and says, "Arise, take possession of the vineyard of Naboth, which he refused to give you for money. I have obtained it for nothing. Naboth is not alive, but dead." And Ahab doesn't question the suspicious circumstances of Naboth's death, he doesn't rebuke Jezebel for her murderous plot, he doesn't allow his conscience to interfere with his covetousness. After all, he didn't kill Naboth. In fact, he doesn't even know how Naboth died, nor does he want to know. All he cares about is that he has his vineyard.

I think there is also something we can learn from Ahab, only it is something to avoid, not imitate. Ahab refused to take appropriate leadership over either his home or his nation. His passivity in the face of Jezebel's heinous sin was itself sinful, for he used her wicked intentions as a convenient cloak to satisfy his own lusts. Rather than providing true leadership through faithfulness and self-sacrifice, Ahab was eager to serve himself at the expense of others. May God help the men in our church to be faithful and godly fathers, husbands, and leaders. But doesn't the moral outrage we feel at the actions of Jezebel and Ahab and the profound compassion we feel for Naboth's family cause us to wonder, "Where is God while all this is happening?" Is He blind that He cannot see? Is

He deaf that He cannot hear? Is He dumb that He cannot speak? Is He paralysed that He cannot move? Where is God?

We might ask the same question today in regard to the evil being perpetrated by a Dictator . . . we see the scenes of starving and hurting mothers and children. Few men are left . . . they have been killed . . . the woman have been raped.

Will God let Ahab and Jezebel, or these other despicable characters escape scot-free after their awful deeds? We shall find the answer as we come to the third scene in our story. As He usually does, God chooses a special instrument to deliver His promise of judgment. That instrument is Elijah, God's prophet, recently recovered from clinical depression and ready to be used again by Almighty God.

Verses 17-29 tell the story. God tells Elijah to go and confront Ahab. Let us not overlook the fact that we have almost no information about Elijah for the 6-10 years since his crash in the Sinai desert. The days passed into months and the months into years, but finally the Word of the Lord comes to Elijah again, telling him to deliver judgment on the House of Ahab. How does Elijah react this time? Does his fear of Jezebel once again drive him into the desert? No, there is no cowardice now, no vacillation, no doubt. His old heroic faith is revived and he immediately proceeds to the vineyard of Naboth and waits there for a classic confrontation.

My imagination tells me that Ahab enters the vineyard and begins to walk down the rows, planning how he will uproot the vines and replace them with herbs and vegetables. As he approaches the end of the plot of ground and turns to go down the last row, a shadow falls in front of him and he shudders as he sees the form of Elijah the Tishbite. He assumed the prophet had died years before in the desert. He hoped against hope that he would never again have to stand before him. But here he is. There is no mistaking this hairy creature with the leather belt about his waist. It is Elijah, God's prophet, in whose place Ahab would rather have seen a whole army marching against him. And Ahab cries out to the prophet, "So you have found me, my enemy!" Did he really think he could hide from Almighty God?

The Psalmist describes as fools those who think the Lord does not see or hear. The writer of Hebrews says, "Nothing in all creation is hidden from God's sight. Everything is uncovered and laid bare before the eyes of Him to whom we must give account." And it's no problem for God to reveal what His eyes see to His prophet. I think it is ironic and tragic how people so often see their true friends as their enemies and their real enemies as their friends.

Teenagers often get angry at their parents and chafe under the rules of the house, though the parents would give their very lives for their children. Yet those same teenagers will believe almost anything their peers say, even though those peers may have no care or concern for their eternal welfare. Church members at times resist the exhortations of their Pastors and Elders, who are committed to their spiritual welfare, and yet will believe anything a TV evangelist tells them, though that evangelist wouldn't have five minutes to give them (unless, of course, they were able to give him a lot of money).

Elijah isn't Ahab's enemy. Ahab is Ahab's enemy. And Jezebel is his enemy. And the false prophets of Baal are his enemy. And covetousness is his enemy. Oh, that we might have divine discernment to know who our real enemies are – those who will lead us away from God and away from righteousness and away from eternal life. Elijah responds to Ahab, "Yes, I have found you, because you have sold yourself to do evil in the eyes of the Lord." Ahab not only did evil; he had sold out to evil. He was a total prisoner of his own lust and covetousness. Elijah delivers a message from God that disaster will come upon Ahab, Jezebel, and their descendants. He tells them they will become dog food. Dogs will lick up Ahab's blood; dogs will devour Jezebel by the wall of Jezreel, and dogs will eat those belonging to Ahab who die in the city, while birds of the air will feed on those who die in the country.

The confrontation between Elijah and Ahab is over. Elijah walks past the stunned King, past his bodyguards, out into the streets of Jezreel and disappears. As far as we know he never sees Ahab again.

Our Chapter ends with an extremely brief biography of Ahab – one of the most tragic epitaphs ever written for a human being. Listen to verse 25 once again: "There was never a man like Ahab, who sold himself to do evil in the eyes of the LORD, urged on by Jezebel his wife."

I wonder if this statement isn't placed right here to teach us a profound and critical lesson – namely that no one, not even the most wicked person on earth, is beyond the reach of God's grace if he will only repent of his sins. For in the next verse we read that Ahab apparently does repent. When Ahab hears Elijah's words he tears his clothes, puts on sackcloth, and begins to fast. I call this an apparent repentance because it is not at all clear how genuine or how permanent it is. In many ways it appears more like remorse, sorrow at getting caught, and regret for the consequences of his actions. But it is this ambiguity regarding Ahab's motives that makes God's grace appear all the more incredible. For the Lord responds favourably to even this hint of repentance on the part of Ahab. It's as though God is so anxious to pardon sinners that He will respond to the faintest sign of spiritual interest.

Don't misunderstand me. I'm not suggesting that if you will just fake a conversion you can fool God. What I am trying to communicate is that God is not an unwilling autocrat who withholds His salvation blessings from all but the most pious and most persistent. You don't have to beat down His door in order to get His attention. If you will but incline your ear to Him, He will respond and give you further opportunity to demonstrate the reality of your faith.

Unfortunately, Ahab doesn't demonstrate much reality to his repentance and eventually the reservoir of God's patience runs dry. And that brings us to the final scene in our story. Chapter 22 opens with the notice that three years have passed since Naboth and his sons were murdered. Ahab is still King of Israel. Jezebel is still Queen. And Naboth's wife, if alive, still suffers from that awful vacuum in her heart. Jezebel probably served Ahab vegetables from Naboth's vineyard, reminding him of that foolish prophet who years before had predicted God's judgment. "Ha, Ahab, I guess the dogs lost the trail." But Ahab probably never heard a dog bark that he didn't jump at.

"It came to pass one day that Ahab solicited the help of Jehoshaphat, King of Judah, to go into battle with him against the King of Aram or Syria. The story of that battle is found in Chapter 22 that you can read about in the next Chapter.

I only draw your attention to the fact that Ahab disguised himself, according to verse 30, because he knew that the Syrians were gunning for him in particular. But he learned that while one can disguise himself from men, one cannot disguise himself from God.

Look at verses 34-38: "But someone drew his bow at random (I think God would put quotes around that word random, for there is nothing truly random in God's plan) and hit the King of Israel between the sections of his armour. The blood from his wound ran onto the floor of the chariot, and that evening he died. He was brought to Samaria, and they buried him there. They washed the chariot at a pool in Samaria (where the prostitutes bathed), and the dogs licked up his blood, as the Word of the LORD had declared."

What about Jezebel?

Some twelve years passed following Ahab's death. Jezebel is still the Queen mother, still flaunting herself against God, still persecuting God's people. Even Elijah has passed off the scene. Have the dogs finally lost the trail? We have to turn over to 2 Kings, Chapter 9 to find out. Again we do not have the space to share the full story – just to note that Jehu has been secretly anointed King of Israel and has been commanded by God to eliminate the House of Ahab.

He went after Jezebel. She is thrown from the Palace window. "Jehu went in and ate and drank. 'Take care of that cursed woman,' he said, 'and bury her, for she was a king's daughter.' But when they went out to bury her, they found nothing except her skull, her feet and her hands. They went back and told Jehu, who said, 'This is the word of the Lord that he spoke through his servant Elijah the Tishbite: On the plot of ground at Jezreel dogs will devour Jezebel's flesh.'" These were tough times.

As a response to this tragic story I would like to suggest four principles.

Principle 1

"Pay-day some-day" is written into the constitution of God's universe. In other words, sin always has its consequences. The Scriptures teach us clearly that "the one who sows to please his sinful nature, from that nature will reap destruction." It also warns, "Do not be deceived. God cannot be mocked. A person reaps what he sows." In a thousand ways the Scripture tells us that "Pay-day some-day" is written into the constitution of God's universe.

Principle 2

The Devil always pays in counterfeit money. The Devil doesn't tempt us with things that are obviously evil so much as he tempts us with things which are good in their place, proper at the right time, honourable with the right person. He does his level best to get us to twist God's Word, to question God's goodness, and to rationalise our disobedience.

The devil's pearls are paste pearls, his diamonds are plastic diamonds, and his nectar is pig food. And if you eat his corn he'll choke you on the cobs. He will. The Devil always pays in counterfeit money.

Principle 3

It is a terrifying thing to fall into the hands of an angry God. That is the testimony of the Word of God as found in Hebrews 10. It's the destiny of all those who sin wilfully in the face of God's revealed will.

The Apostle John wrote, "He who does not obey the Son of God shall not see life, but the wrath of God abides on him." That is, or should be, a terrifying prospect. There will be no arguments at that Great White Throne Judgment, no excuses will be accepted, no rationalizations allowed.

Principle 4

"He who believes in Him is not judged." He who believes in the Son of God has eternal life. If you will but admit your sin before God, acknowledge that Jesus Christ died on Calvary's cross in your place, and receive Him as your personal Saviour, you will never face eternal judgment but rather spend eternity with God in Heaven.

Chapter 7
Ahab and Jehoshaphat
Critical Issues

We have discovered that there is more than just a bunch of ancient Kings in 1 and 2 Kings (with a few dips into Chronicles). These were real people with a real message in their lives for us today. At least, that's how the Bible tells us to view them. We are meant to 'Reign in life' rather than just meander along. By checking out the stories of these Old Testament leaders, we learn a lot about ourselves and how to better relate to God and serve His purposes.

We have checked-out a real mix of characters so far in the previous six chapters. Turning now to 1 Kings 22 and the parallel passage in 2 Chronicles 18, we get a message through a couple of Kings as well as an interesting man of God. Chances are many of you have never heard of Micaiah. We know nothing of his family, his ministry, or his death. Yet the Scriptures tell us enough to know he's the kind of person we would trust with our lives, and he stands on a par with some of God's choicest servants, particularly when it comes to courage and faithfulness.

My approach will be simple – to examine the historical context and evaluate the ministry of Micaiah, and then seek principles for our own lives. 1 Kings 22 says:

"For three years there was no war between Aram and Israel. But in the third year Jehoshaphat king of Judah went down to see the King of Israel *(Ahab).* The King of Israel had said to his officials, "Don't you know that Ramoth Gilead belongs to us and yet we are doing nothing to retake it from the King of Aram?" So he asked Jehoshaphat, "Will you go with me to fight against Ramoth Gilead?" Jehoshaphat replied to the King of Israel, "I am as you are, my people as your people, my horses as your horses." But Jehoshaphat also said to the King of Israel, "First seek the counsel of the LORD."

King Ahab brought together about 400 prophets who said, "Go to war." Jehoshaphat asked if there was anyone else to consult. Micaiah is wheeled in much against Ahab's wish. Ahab reckoned he never got a good word out of him (there were good reasons for that of course knowing what King Ahab was like).

First he tells the King what he wants to hear. "Attack and win". They kind of detect a cynicism in him and say, "Give us the truth." Then we read Micaiah said: "The LORD has put a lying spirit in the mouths of all these prophets of yours. The LORD has decreed disaster for you."

The King says: "Put this fellow in prison and give him nothing but bread and water until I return safely.'" Micaiah declared, "If you ever return safely, the LORD has not spoken through me."

Then he added, "Mark my words, all you people!"

The story of Micaiah comes near the end of Ahab's reign, between the murder of Naboth the Jezreelite and Ahab's death three years later. Our Chapter opens with the notice that three years has passed with no war between Syria and Israel. Israel had won the two previous engagements handily, due to God's sovereign intervention. However, according to Chapter 20, Ahab disobeyed God after capturing the Syrian King, Ben Hadad. Instead of executing him, as God had commanded, Ahab offered to let him go in exchange for the return of some cities the Syrians has captured, and certain trade concessions, like the right to set up Jewish bazaars in the Syrian capital of Damascus. But as soon as Ben Hadad's life was spared he reneged on his agreement and refused to return the occupied territory, including the city of Ramoth-Gilead. That fact seems to be the principal motive for the summit conference we just read about between Ahab and Jehoshaphat, a conference that resulted in: An unwise political alliance.

Just for the sake of reminder, we might mention that these two Kingdoms, Israel and Judah, were formed as the result of a civil war shortly after Solomon's death about a century earlier. Ten of Israel's 12 tribes formed the Northern Kingdom of Israel, of which Ahab is now the eighth King. Two of the tribes – Judah and

Benjamin, formed the Southern Kingdom of Judah, of which Jehoshaphat is the fourth King.

I guess godly kings live longer

Jehoshaphat is one of the few godly Kings of Judah (there were none in Israel), but he had one notable weakness – he was a lover of peace to the point he was willing to compromise to achieve it. The most notable example of this was his arrangement to have Athaliah, the daughter of Ahab and Jezebel, marry his son Jehoram in order to cement a political alliance for the future. Athaliah turned out to be nearly as wicked as her mother and nearly brought about the extermination of the royal family of Judah. Now we find Jehoshaphat agreeing to another, equally unwise, political alliance as he becomes an ally of Ahab against Syria. He had no business doing this because Ahab's political and moral values were so very different from his own. But besides being an unwise political alliance, this was also an unholy religious alliance.

These two Kings reigned simultaneously for twenty years, but they were cut out of very different cloth. Ahab was a wicked King, actually encouraging idolatry among his people, while Jehoshaphat was essentially a good King, whose few recorded sins include the fact that he hobnobbed with Ahab.

But why shouldn't they have this summit conference, and why shouldn't they be at peace with one another? Aren't they both Jews? That's Jehoshaphat's contention in verse 4: "I am as you are, my people as your people, my horses as your horses." Yes, racially they were both Israelites, but certainly not spiritually. As the Apostle Paul wrote centuries later, "He is a Jew who is one inwardly." And Ahab was certainly not a Jew by that criterion.

2 Corinthians 6:14-16 speaks very pointedly to us about the danger of an unequal yoke: "Do not be yoked together with unbelievers. For what do righteousness and wickedness have in common? Or what fellowship can light have with darkness? What does a believer have in common with an unbeliever? What agreement is there between the temple of God and idols? Therefore, come out from them and be separate."

Now this passage cannot be interpreted as forbidding all co-operation and interaction between believers and unbelievers, for the Scriptures clearly indicate we are to be in the world but not of the world. And sometimes it is difficult to determine whether a certain kind of alliance with unbelievers is wise or foolish, holy or unholy. We need God's wisdom as well as His Word in such situations. But God is certainly not pleased with this unholy alliance and I believe Jehoshaphat knows he is in dangerous territory, and that is why he suggests in verse 5, almost as an afterthought, "First seek the counsel of the LORD."

I'm sure Ahab wasn't pleased with this suggestion. But I fault Jehoshaphat more, because he should have known better than to wait until this point to ask God. But do you ever find yourself doing the same thing? You lay your plans, you make key decisions, and then it suddenly occurs that you need to ask God to endorse your plans. So you ask, "Lord, is this what you want me to do? It must be, because I've already committed myself. Now will you bless the results?"

Ahab responds to Jehoshaphat's suggestion by rounding up 400 prophets to ascertain God's will in the matter. Are these prophets of Baal, supported and sponsored by his wife Jezebel – replacements for the 400 prophets of Baal whom Elijah killed after the battle of Mt. Carmel? I hardly think Jehoshaphat would have tolerated the presence of prophets of Baal. Besides, the one prophet of these 400 who is named, Zedekiah, has a name which means, "the righteousness of Yahweh," implying that he at least professes to be a true prophet of the Lord.

I think it more likely that these 400 prophets are the establishment Jewish religious leaders, tolerated by Ahab primarily because they seldom give him any trouble. They are like the spiritual leaders of whom Paul spoke when he said, "They have a form of godliness but deny the power thereof."

Responding to Ahab's request for confirmation from the Lord as to whether to go up to battle, these prophets respond with enthusiasm, "Go for it, Ahab, for the Lord will give you victory." That's exactly what Ahab wants to hear and he's delighted, for now Jehoshaphat should have no hesitation about joining him in taking on Syria. But then Jehoshaphat expresses some lingering doubts: "Is there not yet a prophet of the LORD here whom we may inquire of?"

What do you suppose raises suspicion in Jehoshaphat's mind that Ahab's prophets may not be speaking for God? Perhaps it is the fact that someone with Ahab's reputation could get such quick and unanimous approval. Or perhaps it is one of the words these prophets use. In verse 6 they use the term "Lord" but it is a different word in Hebrew than Jehoshaphat used in verse 7. He used "Yahweh," the personal Name for Israel's God, while they use "Adonai," the more formal Name. It's like the difference between saying "my Father" and "God." Maybe they give themselves away by their hesitancy to use God's personal Name.

Now with that as historical background, we are ready to meet Micaiah, God's prophet, who has an incredible reputation for honesty and integrity.

Ahab condemns himself with his attitude toward Micaiah. Look again at verse 8: "The King of Israel answered Jehoshaphat, 'There is still one man through whom we can inquire of the Lord, but I hate him because he never prophesies anything good about me, but always bad. He is Micaiah son of Imlah.'"

Yes, there is one prophet who can tell you what Yahweh says. What a sad commentary on the spiritual condition of his Kingdom that there is only one who can be counted on to speak for God. But at least there is one. His reputation for truthfulness is Micaiah's greatest asset. The fact that Ahab hates him is also a pretty good indication of his godly character. But it's not just Ahab who condemns himself with this attitude toward Micaiah. I believe Jehoshaphat also condemns himself with his wimpy response to Ahab.

Jehoshaphat condemns himself with his mild rebuke of Ahab. He responds by saying in effect, "Naughty, naughty, Ahab. You shouldn't say such things about Micaiah. You shouldn't hate anybody." I'm being a bit sarcastic because one could have hoped for a more forthright response from Jehoshaphat. Ahab's attitude toward this true prophet should have been a dead giveaway to Jehoshaphat and should have sent him hightailing it back to Jerusalem. But he doesn't, so Ahab calls for Micaiah.

We find the two Kings sitting on their portable thrones near the gate of Samaria, dressed up in their royal regalia. All the establishment prophets are prophesying and their leader, Zedekiah, is using a visual aid to get his point across. He has made a couple of iron horns and uses them to illustrate how Israel will gore the Syrians and defeat them. Meanwhile the messenger sent to summon Micaiah (apparently from prison), is filling the prophet in on what's happening and encouraging him not to rain on Ahab's parade. "Micaiah, don't make waves. Everyone is agreed we should go into battle, and you will be odd-man-out unless you join them." But Micaiah responds, "As surely as the Lord lives, I can tell him only what the Lord tells me." Wow! That's the kind of courage and integrity we love to see. But then in verse 15 we begin to wonder whether this man's reputation for honesty is entirely deserved. In fact, Micaiah, God's honest prophet, "lies" to both of them. Ahab asks him, "Micaiah, shall we go to war against Ramoth Gilead, or shall I refrain?" and he agrees immediately with the judgment of the other 400 prophets: "Attack and be victorious, for the LORD will give it into the King's hand."

But immediately Ahab smells a rat. Never before has Micaiah had anything positive to say to Ahab and, besides, I suspect Micaiah's tone of voice betrays a distinct lack of sincerity. It's as though Micaiah responded, "Sure Ahab, God will give you anything you want because you're such a devoted follower of His."

Knowing in his heart that the prophet is pulling his leg, Ahab screams at Micaiah, "How many times must I make you swear to tell me nothing but the truth in the Name of the Lord?" He's furious. He doesn't really want to know the truth (or he wouldn't have chased the true prophets out of Israel), but he doesn't like being toyed with either. In the next scene we discover that Micaiah delivers on his reputation for honesty and integrity. He responds to Ahab, "Okay, you want the truth, I'll give you the hard, unadulterated truth." And he reveals a vision the Lord has given him, a vision that begins, "I saw the Lord sitting on His throne with all the Host of Heaven standing around Him on His right and on His left."

The two rich and powerful Kings before him are sitting on their thrones in all the royal splendour they can muster, but friends, when you have seen God on His Throne, you are not impressed or threatened by an Ahab or a Jehoshaphat sitting on theirs.

The vision shows an army in disarray. The Commander-in-Chief is dead, and the leaderless people are in retreat to their homes. That, says, Micaiah, will be the end result if Ahab and Jehoshaphat go into battle against Syria. Ahab turns to Jehoshaphat: "I knew it. I told you so, didn't I? He never prophesies anything good about me, but only bad." But Micaiah continues, revealing the fundamental reason why the score is 400 to 1. He explains to us once for all why truth cannot be established by majority vote. It all has to do with spiritual warfare invisible to human eyes. Micaiah reveals the truth about spiritual warfare. He tells us about a meeting going on up in Heaven. God is looking for a spirit messenger to entice Ahab to launch the battle in which he will be killed.

Look again at verse 21. Finally, a spirit came forward, stood before the Lord and said, "I will entice him." "By what means?" the Lord asked. "I will go out and be a lying spirit in the mouths of all his prophets," he said. "You will succeed in enticing him," said the Lord. "Go and do it."

I see several important truths here that we must grasp about spiritual warfare

First: God is deeply involved in human affairs. In fact, He is in control of His entire universe. Not even political evil and religious apostasy are outside His knowledge and His sovereignty. While Ahab is plotting military strategy, God is planning the end of Ahab.

Second: God can employ evil as well as good instruments to accomplish His purposes, while never Himself committing evil or approving the evil. He can use an evil angel as well as a good one; He can use a wicked nation as well as a righteous one. This bothers some of us, but we're not in bad company – it also bothered the prophet Habakkuk. He didn't appreciate it one bit when God raised up the Chaldeans to punish the Jews because, though the Jews certainly deserved to be punished, the Chaldeans were even worse. He chided God for being "silent while the wicked swallow up those more righteous than themselves?" And how did God answer? "Don't worry about it. If I decide to use the wicked, that's My business. But it still doesn't excuse the Chaldeans. Someday they will get theirs." God can use any instrument He chooses to accomplish His purposes. In this case He uses an evil spirit to deceive the prophets, who in turn deceive Ahab.

Third: Satanic blindness covers the eyes of those who do not believe, resulting in incredible darkness. While there are countless examples of this in the Bible, I think it most worthwhile to turn directly to 2 Corinthians 4:4: "The god of this age has blinded the minds of unbelievers, so that they cannot see the light of the Gospel of the glory of Christ, who is the image of God." And in 2 Thessalonians 2:11,12 the influence of Anti-Christ in the end times is described this way: "God sends them a powerful delusion so that they will believe the lie and so that all will be condemned who have not believed the truth but have delighted in wickedness."

In 1 Kings 22 we see a clear illustration of how this Satanic blindness operates. But I want to take a risk and apply this to the ecclesiastical situation in our day. In my country there are thousand of church buildings. I would estimate that in a large majority of these churches the Gospel of Jesus Christ is not preached so that people can be saved and nurtured in their faith. Why? Are those clergy purposely deceiving their people in order to lead them astray? No, of course not. They are themselves victims of a deceptive plan by which Satan is leading both clergy and people astray. Many religious leaders (and this was just as true in Jesus' day as it is today) are sincere but sincerely wrong; they are blind guides of the blind. And that is why Micaiah is standing alone. He is the only one whom the evil spirit has not been able to seduce. Happily in my country there are a number of churches in a variety of denominations which do preach the true Gospel, though I sadly suspect they are still a distinct minority.

So far we have seen that Micaiah has a reputation for honesty and integrity, and that he has delivered on his reputation. Now we see finally that he must pay the consequences for his honesty and integrity. Sometimes God rewards His faithful servants immediately for acts of courage. But at other times the rewards are deferred. Micaiah's rewards are deferred. In the meantime he begins to pay the consequences for being truthful.

The first of these is enduring the anger of the other prophets.

Verse 24 says that Zedekiah, the leader of the four hundred deceived prophets, approaches Micaiah and slaps him in the face. This action provides some important insight into human nature. When someone tells us something we don't want to hear and we know down deep we're wrong, how do we react? Often in anger, don't we? In fact, anger and bitterness are frequently a sign of insecurity and guilt. But when we know we're in the right and are falsely accused, it is much easier to respond with calm and even pity towards our accuser, confident that the truth will vindicate itself, confident that God will vindicate us. Think about that the next time you're tempted to slug someone, either physically or verbally, because they told you something you didn't want to hear.

Zedekiah doesn't just strike Micaiah – he also asks him a question: "How did the Spirit of the Lord pass from me to speak to you?" In other words, "Prove that you're telling the truth and we're all deceived." Micaiah's answer is simply, "Wait and see. You'll find out on the day you have to find a hiding place." In other words, "After Ahab is killed in the forthcoming battle and the army returns home in disarray, there's going to be a bounty out on you prophets who promised victory. Then you will realize I was telling the truth."

Zedekiah is not the only one to bring consequences to bear upon Micaiah for his honesty. In verses 26 and 27 we read that the King orders him to be returned to prison and placed on survival rations until he returns safely. To which Micaiah confidently responds, "If you do return safely, then the Lord has not spoken by me." And with that he turns and addresses the people, "Mark my words, all you people!" He is not hesitant to call the whole nation to witness the outcome – hopefully many people will turn to God in repentance. And that's the last we hear of Micaiah. We don't know whether he died in prison or was released following Ahab's death. We do know, however, that he trusted in God, and God has promised to reward His faithful servants, either in this life or the next.

Before concluding with some important practical principles which we can apply to our own lives, perhaps a brief postscript is in order regarding the outcome of our story. Despite Micaiah's warning Ahab and Jehoshaphat went ahead with their battle plans against the Syrians at Ramoth-Gilead. Ahab thought he could protect himself by wearing a disguise in battle, but a certain archer drew his bow at random and struck the king of Israel in a joint of his armour. He died that evening, and the dogs licked his blood as the prophet Elijah had predicted years earlier. Jehoshaphat himself was saved only by the skin of his teeth and was rebuked strongly by one of God's prophets for disobeying the Word of the Lord. We read of this rebuke in 2 Chronicles 19:1-3: "Jehu the prophet said to King Jehoshaphat: 'Should you help the wicked and love those who hate the Lord and so bring wrath on yourself from the Lord? But there is some good in you, for you have removed the idols from the land and you have set your heart to seek God."

Here are some principles to ponder and pursue.

First: God's faithful servants are always in the minority

Nothing should be more clear from the Word of God than this: if you speak the truth, if you live for Christ, if you take a stand for righteousness, you're going to be in the minority, and probably in a very small minority. You'll be different, you may be laughed at, you may be hated. Remember that Jesus said, "Don't be surprised if the world hates you. It hated Me before it hated you."

If you're out in the work-a-day world and refuse to swear, expect to be in the minority. If you're in school and you refuse to laugh or even to listen to dirty jokes, expect to be in the minority. If you live faithfully with your spouse, expect to be in the minority. If you spend a quiet time with God each day and get into a small group, expect to be in the minority. If you give regularly as God has blessed you in the support of God's Work, expect to be in the minority. And if you serve God unselfishly in His Church, expect to be in the minority. God's faithful servants are always in the minority.

Second: God's faithful servants have reputations for honesty and righteousness, even among their enemies.

It is one thing to have a good reputation among your friends and fellow church members. It's another thing to have the same among your enemies. Ahab said of Micaiah, "I hate him because he always tells the truth about me." How many of God's enemies hate you because your walk is so consistent that you bring conviction on them every time they're around you?

Third: God's faithful servants have boldness and confidence in the Lord.

Micaiah is a great example in that he didn't confer with flesh and blood, he didn't waver, and he didn't consider the negative consequences to himself, but rather boldly spoke and lived the truth, come what may. You know, God is still looking for men and women and young people to stand boldly for the truth.

Back in 1994 Mother Teresa was invited to speak at the National Prayer Breakfast in Washington DC. US President Clinton and his wife were sitting on the front row, and many cabinet members and political leaders from the Administration were present as well as political leaders and other influential guests from around the world. There were a number of topics Mother Teresa could have addressed that would have generated accolades from the powers that be – she could have spoken of the power of prayer or the need to love one another or the goodness of America – everyone would have eaten that up. But instead she focused her remarks on the last, the least, and the lost. She spoke with power and conviction: "I feel that the greatest destroyer of peace today is abortion, because it is a war against the child, a direct killing of the innocent child, murder by the mother herself. And if we accept that a mother can kill even her own child, how can we tell other people not to kill one another? Please don't kill the child. I want the child. Please give me the child. I am willing to accept any child who would be aborted and to give that child to a married couple who will love the child and be loved by the child. From our children's home in Calcutta alone, we have saved over 3000 children from abortion. These children have brought such love and joy to their adopting parents and have grown up so full of love and joy."

That, is a great example of the kind of honesty and integrity we need today. God's call on your life may be different to Mother Teresa's, but whatever that call is, it will require courage and fortitude and honesty.

As a matter of fact, even more important than being honest about abortion is the need to be honest about the lost condition of people all around us and the fact that Jesus is the only Way to God. Our culture doesn't want to hear that, but it needs to hear it. It needs to hear that sins are forgiven only at the Cross. If you take a stand on truth, you are going to be the odd-man-out; you are going to be unappreciated, unpopular, perhaps even persecuted. Yet that is what God is calling us to do. It is not peace at all costs; it is truth at all costs. May God find us faithful.

Chapter 8
Jehoshaphat
The Battle Is Not Yours

Parents are choosing Bible names for their children in record numbers. In a survey Michael was the most popular, but others frequently chosen were Joshua, Mary, Elizabeth, Timothy, David, Andrew, and Matthew. Generally the more godly and successful the person was in Bible times; the more popular the name is today. Little wonder, then, that Ahab, Jezebel and Judas are rarely, if ever, chosen. But one name that doesn't fit this particular pattern is Jehoshaphat. He ranks right up there with the best of the individuals in terms of character and contribution, but his name isn't on anyone's most popular list. I don't understand – it must be for the same reason that Methuselah and Mephibosheth are missing (try getting your tongue round them fast - it's not easy), but why Jehoshaphat? Is it the same kind of reason? I want to put Jehoshaphat's life into proper historical context and then to examine in some detail what was perhaps the greatest military victory in the history of Israel. In the process we should gain some significant insight into how and why God comes to the rescue of His people when they are in distress.

Earlier in this book we considered Asa, a King of Judah whose epitaph was that "he did not seek help from the Lord, but only from the physicians." Asa was, for the most part, a good King, and Jehoshaphat was his son and successor. The two of them were on the throne of the Southern Kingdom of Judah for a combined 60 plus years. All the other individuals whose epitaphs we have examined in this series – from Ahab and Jezebel, to Micaiah, including prophets like Elijah, Elisha, and Naaman – were contemporary with these two Kings, except that these others were connected with the Northern kingdom of Israel.

In 2 Chronicles 17:3-6 we read this statement about Jehoshaphat after he succeeded his father Asa as King of Judah. "The Lord was with Jehoshaphat because in his early years he walked in the ways his father David had followed. He did not consult the Baals but sought the God of his father and followed His commands rather than the practices of Israel. The Lord established the Kingdom under his control; and all Judah brought gifts to Jehoshaphat, so that he had great wealth and honour. His heart was devoted to the ways of the Lord."

Do you notice the cause and effect statements there? "The Lord was with Jehoshaphat because he walked in the ways of David . . . The Lord established the Kingdom under his control . . . so that he had great wealth and honour." God's continued blessings are always contingent on obedience. Furthermore, peace and prosperity are gifts that come from the Lord. We must never forget that. I was struck by the

Fourth of July celebrations I witnessed when in America for a preaching tour. Can you believe it. I, an Englishman, was the guest speaker at a number of events. At the civil ceremonies no effort was made to hide the nation's dependence upon God. In fact, among the songs that received top billing at these celebrations were 'God Bless America', and even *'Amazing Grace'* – God was invoked constantly in music and the spoken word, and He was rightly referred to as the foundation of all freedoms. I only wish the display of civil religion, which I have seen in so many countries, was translated into the daily lives of the people. It was for Jehoshaphat.

In Chapter 17 it goes on to say that in the third year of his reign Jehoshaphat began a biblical education campaign throughout the country. He commissioned key officials and priests and Levites to teach the Book of the Law of the Lord (probably the Pentateuch, the first five books of the Old Testament) to all the towns of Judah. The result was that the fear of the Lord fell on the people and on all the surrounding countries – so much so that they ceased hostilities toward Judah. Some even brought gifts and silver and flocks to Jehoshaphat so that he became more and more prosperous and powerful. God's blessing was very evident on this godly king. But Jehoshaphat then went through a period of independence like many of us have gone through or may be currently going through. He forgot where his power and wealth originated.

He began to look to his own resources and ingenuity. You will perhaps recall from 2 Chronicles Chapter 18, the story of Micaiah, that Jehoshaphat allied himself with Ahab by marriage, arranging for his son Jehoram to marry Athaliah, the daughter of Ahab and Jezebel. Then he visited Ahab in his Capital of Samaria, and agreed to go into battle with him to help him recapture the city of Ramoth Gilead, which had been seized by the Syrians.

Jehoshaphat valued peace with his neighbour to the north; unfortunately, he valued it so much that he was at times willing to compromise his principles to achieve it. He almost lost his life in that particular military alliance with Ahab, and God rebuked him through the prophet Jehu: "Should you help the wicked and love those who hate the Lord? Because of this, the wrath of the Lord is upon you. There is, however, some good in you, for you have rid the land of the Asherah poles and have set your heart on seeking God."

His devotion was not merely outward, for show, but stemmed from deep within. He made some serious mistakes, but like David his heart was generally set on God. You know the statement from 1 Peter 4:8: "Love covers a multitude of sins"? So does a heart set on seeking God. Jehoshaphat took the rebuke of the prophet to heart, God gave him a reprieve, and so, not surprisingly, we learn next of his most significant leadership contribution. He set up a judicial system patterned somewhat after that Moses instituted over 600 years earlier. It can be stated without fear of contradiction that no nation will ever rise above its judicial system.

A country's leadership can be evil and even tyrannical, but if the judicial system remains intact, the country will stand. A nation's legislature can be incompetent and corrupt, but if the judiciary is solid, the nation will survive. You see, the judicial branch of government in a democracy is the most critical, for while governments can be voted out of office and legislators can be replaced, judges serve with a measure of independence.

Jehoshaphat knew how important judges are to a nation's health, so he went out among the people, turned them back to the Lord, and appointed godly judges in each of the fortified cities. Here are the instructions he gave them: "Consider carefully what you do, because you are not judging for man but for the Lord, who is with you whenever you give a verdict. Now let the fear of the Lord be upon you. Judge carefully, for with the Lord our God there is no injustice or partiality or bribery."

He takes their job description back to the nature and character of God. Because there is no injustice or partiality or bribery with God, there should be none with them. They do not work for the King or for the nation; they ultimately work for a just and holy God.

Jehoshaphat set up administrative small claims courts to handle disputes between individuals, disputes that perhaps weren't serious enough to have to go before a judge. To handle these issues he appointed Levites, priests and heads of families. Here again honesty and integrity were essential. Listen to Jehoshaphat's instructions to those involved in these family courts: "You must serve faithfully and wholeheartedly in the fear of the Lord. In every case that comes before you from your fellow countrymen who live in the cities . . . you are to warn them not to sin against the Lord; otherwise His wrath will come on you and your brothers. Do this, and you will not sin."

The importance of this historical background is that all of this sets the stage for the most important event in Jehoshaphat's reign – a battle that is described in detail in 2 Chronicles 20. This battle resulted in the greatest victory that Israel ever accomplished. It is much greater than the conquest of Palestine, the victory over Jericho, or any of the other victories recorded in Scripture, because it is used again in Scripture as a symbol of the final battle, Armageddon, on the Great Day of the Lord, when the Lord will deliver His people. In fact, the valley of Har Meggido *(Armageddon)* is also called in Scripture The Valley of Jehoshaphat. What we must realize, however, is that this great victory was not obtained in isolation from the rest of Jehoshaphat's life. I believe it was because he sought the Lord, because he repented of his compromising with Ahab, and because he built a judicial system based on integrity that God gave him this great victory.

It all begins with a sudden and unprecedented threat. In verse 2 we read, "Some men came and told Jehoshaphat, 'A vast army is coming against you from Edom, from the other side of the Sea (the Dead Sea). It is already in Hazazon Tamar (essentially a day's march away)."

God had used Jehoshaphat to bring about a significant spiritual revival in Israel. The nation was enjoying the fruits of that revival – peace and prosperity – when suddenly they were attacked by enemies from across the Jordan. That's the way it often seems to happen. We're going along pursuing what we believe to be the right course, God is blessing our socks off, and then with no warning we are suddenly attacked – perhaps by an illness, a job loss, a broken relationship, or a death in the family. At the very time when we expect things to go well, everything begins to come apart. Why? C.S. Lewis, in his greatest masterpiece, *The Problem of Pain,* offers a great deal of wisdom on this subject. He writes: "We are perplexed to see misfortune falling upon decent, inoffensive, worthy people – on capable, hard working mothers of families or diligent, thrifty little trades-people, on those who have worked so hard, and so honestly, for their modest stock of happiness and now seem to be entering on the enjoyment of it with the fullest right . . . Let me implore the reader to try to believe, if only for the moment, that God, who made these deserving people, may really be right when He thinks that their modest prosperity and the happiness of their children are not enough to make them blessed; that all this must fall from them in the end, and that if they have not learned to know Him they will be wretched. And therefore He troubles them, warning them in advance of an insufficiency that one day they will have to discover." "Pain," he writes later, "is the megaphone God uses to get our attention."

He sure got Jehoshaphat's attention, and I think it is fairly obvious that Jehoshaphat and his people come to know God better because of this threat than they would have had it not happened. And so what is Jehoshaphat's reaction to this threat to his nation? I characterise it as fear followed by faith.

First, he is "alarmed," according to verse 3. He's scared witless. He knows he doesn't have the resources to meet this attack from the hordes across the Jordan. But let's not be unnecessarily critical of Jehoshaphat here. Fear in a situation like this is only natural, and it is not wrong. "It is not the initial reaction of fear which matters; it is what we do with that fear." When Jesus said to His disciples, *"Fear not,"* he used a present tense – "Do not keep on fearing." It would be foolish to tell someone not to be afraid initially when they face some unexpected threat, but it is foolish to tell them they should keep on fearing.

What do you do with fear? Does it cause you to run and hide? Does it make you angry and irritable? Does it drive you to drink or to eat or to some other addiction? Or does fear drive you to the Lord? Well, let's see where it took Jehoshaphat.

Verse 3 goes on, "Alarmed, Jehoshaphat resolved to inquire of the Lord, and he proclaimed a fast for all Judah. The people of Judah came together to seek help from the Lord; indeed, they came from every town in Judah to seek Him." I don't think it's any accident that the term "resolved" is used here. When you're frightened to death, your emotions cannot help you. You have to win a victory over your emotions with your mind and will. You have to go back to what you know is the truth and resolve to do the right thing. And the right thing for a time like this is to seek the Lord. Jeremiah records this truth best: "'You will seek Me and find Me when you seek Me with all your heart. I will be found by you,' declares the Lord."

Fasting is a spiritual discipline that in the Old Testament was often employed in times of national emergency or personal trial. On rare occasions, as here, the people of God were called upon to fast corporately. The purpose of fasting was to allow the people to focus all their energies upon seeking the face of God. Most of us don't realise how much of our day is given to food – thinking about food, preparing food, eating food, cleaning up afterward, and then finding a snack. Right? I think that's why fasting played a fairly prominent role in biblical spirituality; if we can simply get away from our fixation on food, our attention can be directed more toward God. And frankly, it doesn't hurt a person to go without food occasionally, providing one doesn't have a medical condition that would be aggravated by it.

I read these comments published in medical journals. It presented dramatic evidence that fasting is actually beneficial to the body, for example in lowering cholesterol. Therefore, it is undoubtedly a spiritual discipline that more believers should incorporate into their lives. There is a specific danger related to fasting, however, and that danger is probably why there is so little mention of fasting in the New Testament, and virtually none in the Epistles – and that is spiritual pride. Jesus warned in the Sermon on the Mount, "When you fast, do not look sombre as the hypocrites do, for they disfigure their faces to show men they are fasting. I tell you the truth, they have received their reward in full. But when you fast, put oil on your head and wash your face, so that it will not be obvious to men that you are fasting, but only to your Father, who is unseen; and your Father, who sees what is done in secret, will reward you."

Fasting is one of those disciplines that can easily become a badge of honour. In fact, there have been a few high profile Christian leaders in recent years that have gone on extended fasts and urged their followers to do likewise. I have something of a problem with that – if someone wants to go on a 40-day fast, that's fine, but it should be between them and the Lord, not for public bragging rights. I might also mention that fasting from food may not be the only option for believers to consider. I suspect there are those who need to occasionally fast from TV or from sports or from anything that tends to consume their time and attention. In Scripture fasting is almost always accompanied by prayer; in fact, it is done for the purpose of focused prayer. Certainly that is true in this case.

Jehoshaphat stands up before all the people at the Temple in Jerusalem and prays a powerful prayer. Listen to his words: "O Lord, God of our fathers, are you not the God who is in Heaven? You rule over all the kingdoms of the nations. Power and might are in your hand, and no one can withstand you. O our God, did you not drive out the inhabitants of this land before your people Israel and give it forever to the descendants of Abraham your friend? They have lived in it and have built in it a sanctuary for your Name, saying, "If calamity comes upon us, whether the sword of judgment, or plague or famine, we will stand in Your presence before this Temple that bears your Name and will cry out to You in our distress, and You will hear us and save us." But now here are men from Ammon, Moab and Mount Seir, whose territory you would not allow Israel to invade when they came from Egypt; so they turned away from them and did not destroy them. See how they are repaying us by coming to drive us out of the possession You gave us as an inheritance. O our God, will You not judge them? For we have no power to face this vast army that is attacking us. We do not know what to do, but our eyes are upon You."

Notice the pattern of Jehoshaphat's prayer. He starts with who God is, then what God has done, then what God has promised, and finally, on the basis of all that, he relates what his people need. He is the LORD, the personal covenant-keeping God, the God of their fathers, the God who is in Heaven. But He is not just in Heaven; He is the Ruler over all the nations of the earth. He is the Ruler over the Ammonites and the Moabites and the Edomites. He is Ruler over Iran, Iraq, and Afghanistan. He is Ruler over the Internet and global business monopolies. He rules over your family, your circumstances, and your investments. He is sovereign; He is in control; He is without equal. No one ever has or will ever block His will. That is why we can go to Him confidently in prayer.

The primary Work of God which Jehoshaphat focuses on is the conquest of Palestine. It happened by God's hands, for He is the One who drove out the inhabitants of the land and gave it forever to the descendants of Abraham.

You know, the Nation of Israel is one of the oddities of history. There is simply no way to explain the continuance of that Nation apart from some kind of divine intervention. For almost three and a half millennia there has been a Nation identified as Israel, and though they have waxed and waned, at times almost disappearing, they always survive. Jesus said that their continuance is linked with that of the sun and the moon. As long as there is a sun in the sky, and as long as the moon appears at night, there will be a Nation of Israel. If you ever wake up some morning, and the sun doesn't rise, then it's time to worry about Israel's survival, but not until!

Then, Jehoshaphat goes back in history to the dedication of the Temple, when God said to Solomon: "My eyes will be open and My ears attentive to the prayers offered in this place." Jehoshaphat claims that promise because it is as good in Jehoshaphat's day as it was in Solomon's. And it's just as good today. The promises of God are sure and certain; when we cry out to Him in our distress, He will hear us and save us – not just from our problems but also from our sins.

Now on the basis of who God is, what He has done, and what He has promised, Jehoshaphat is ready to make his request. He rehearses the threat of the armies facing them, and then in verse 12 he lays the real issue on the table: "O our God, will you not judge them? For we have no power to face this vast army that is attacking us. We do not know what to do, but our eyes are upon You."

That is the bottom line. There are many times when we do not know what to do, but if our eyes are upon the Lord, if we are trusting in Him to help us, we will see the goodness of the Lord in the land of the living, as Job put it. And even if He chooses not to do what we want Him to do, or if His timetable is different from ours, our eyes should remain on Him, for He is completely trustworthy.

Remember what the three Hebrew children, Shadrach, Meshach and Abednego, said as they faced the fiery furnace? "O Nebuchadnezzar, we do not need to defend ourselves before you in this matter. If we are thrown into the blazing furnace, the God we serve is able to save us from it, and He will rescue us from your hand, O king. But even if he does not, we want you to know, O king, that we will not serve your gods or worship the image of gold you have set up." They well knew that God was their only hope. If He didn't come through, it could only be because He had better plans.

The prayer of Jehoshaphat was heard by the entire nation, the men, their wives, and their children; even their babies are mentioned. All of them witnessed the faith of the King. Then the Spirit of the Lord came upon a prophet named Jahaziel and he gave God's response to the King's prayer: "Listen, King Jehoshaphat and all who live in Judah and Jerusalem! This is what the Lord says to you: "Do not be afraid or discouraged because of this vast army. For the battle is not yours but God's. Tomorrow march down against them. They will be climbing up by the Pass of Ziz, and you will find them at the end of the gorge in the Desert of Jeruel. You will not have to fight this battle. Take up your positions; stand firm and see the deliverance the Lord will give you, O Judah and Jerusalem. Do not be afraid; do not be discouraged. Go out to face them tomorrow, and the Lord will be with you."

The theology here is the same as that of 1 Samuel 17:47 when the young shepherd boy David went up against the Philistine giant, Goliath. David said to the Philistines, "All those gathered here will know that it is not by sword or spear that the Lord saves; for the battle is the LORD's and He will give all of you into our hands."

I want you to notice something very interesting. While the prophet tells the people that the battle is not theirs but God's, he nevertheless orders them to march against the enemy. He tells them they will not have to fight, but he also orders them to take up their positions and to stand firm. I suggest that there's a nearly universal principle here: The spiritual life is not a passive life – *"just let go and let God."* It's an active life wherein the believer is engaged, employing the gifts and abilities and stamina and energy he has, which God then directs and empowers. Even in the rare situation where God achieves the victory completely by His own actions, as here, still He requires His people to prepare for battle and to stand firm.

On occasions I find a person who is out of work, and he says he is trusting God to find him a job. But he isn't sending out resumes or networking or hitting the streets. Now I realise he could be depressed, especially if he's been out of work for some time. But I think he will much more likely see the hand of God moving in his behalf and answering his prayer if he's engaged with God in the process. The same is true when dealing with medical or emotional problems. We need to be involved in our own treatment – taking the medicine that is indicated, getting exercise, watching our diets – and God will often work through those means to heal us.

Evangelicals have been known to mock the old saying, "God helps those who help themselves," (which, in a recent survey was thought by most people to be a biblical quote, but of course it is not). We mock because it seems to some to go against our theology of grace. I understand that. Ultimately God helps those who can't help themselves, because there is no way anyone can work his way to Heaven. But there is truth as well in the fact that God expects His people to be actively engaged in the spiritual battle – in life and faith and ministry and healing. It's kind of like the old golfer saying, "The guys who work the hardest seem to have the most luck."

"At the prophet's words Jehoshaphat bows with his face to the ground, and all the people fall down in worship before the Lord. Then some of the Levites spontaneously begin to praise the Lord with a very loud voice. Early the next morning they leave for the Desert of Tekoa to do as the Lord instructed them. Jehoshaphat stands before the people and says, "Listen to me, Judah and people of Jerusalem! Have faith in the LORD your God and you will be upheld; have faith in His prophets and you will be successful."

Why do you think he mentions faith in the Lord and faith in the prophets? I think it's because it is through the prophets that God's will is made known to His people. There are many today who speak glibly about faith in God but they reject nearly everything His prophets have said in the Bible.

There is a famine in the church today, not unlike that predicted by the prophet Amos: "'The days are coming,' declares the Sovereign LORD, 'When I will send a famine through the land – not a famine of food or a thirst for water, but a famine of hearing the Words of the LORD'." The church is suffering spiritual malnutrition because many of the shepherds of God's flock are not feeding the sheep.

The praise does not stop, for Jehoshaphat also appoints a men's choir to lead the army, and they sing, "Give thanks to the Lord, for his love endures forever." And, according to verse 22, "as they began to sing and praise," the Lord sets ambushes against their enemies and they are defeated. The enemies of Israel begin to fight one another and totally annihilate one another.

The key weapons of Israel were praise and worship. I wonder if God didn't intend for those to be our key weapons as well. There's something about a heart of worship that is able to deflect all spiritual attacks of the Enemy. The extent of Jehoshaphat's victory is recounted for us in verse 24: "When the men of Judah came to the place that overlooks the desert and looked toward the vast army, they saw only dead bodies lying on the ground; no one had escaped. So Jehoshaphat and his men went to carry off their plunder, and they found among them a great amount of equipment and clothing and also articles of value – more than they could take away. There was so much plunder that it took three days to collect it."

Every major victory in the Bible downplays the human factor and exalts the action of God. And I believe the principle still stands today: if we want to see a great movement of the power of God, we'd better get out of the way. We tend to put so much stock in methods and programmes and preparation and performance – sometimes there's no room left for the miraculous *(or even for providence).* The last scene is one of joy and peace. Look at the conclusion of the story: "Then, led by Jehoshaphat, all the men of Judah and Jerusalem returned joyfully to Jerusalem, for the Lord had given them cause to rejoice over their enemies. They entered Jerusalem and went to the Temple of the Lord with harps and lutes and trumpets. The fear of God came upon all the kingdoms of the countries when they heard how the Lord had fought against the enemies of Israel. And the Kingdom of Jehoshaphat was at peace, for his God had given him rest on every side."

Do you see the terms repeated there: joyfully, rejoice; peace, rest. Those are the results when we put our trust in the Lord. Alarm was the initial reaction to the threat; now the people are full of joy and experiencing peace because of God's intervention. There's the story of Jehoshaphat: Unprecedented threat, fear followed by faith, praise and worship, victory and reward, joy and peace. Frankly, I believe Jehoshaphat's experience should be the norm, not the exception for believers, and it can be. We need to realise that whatever present disaster we may be facing, though it is different from a king facing a threatening army, the emotional effect of fear is the same. But the solution is also the same. As God helped Jehoshaphat when the King sought Him, so He can and will help you. Seek Him with all your heart.

Chapter 9
Joash
Giving Up And Given Up

When I was a Church Pastor I remember a number of discussions we had among the Church Leadership about mentoring a younger generation. I was very keen to help equip a younger crowd for leadership. I have thought for a long time that youth is not the church of tomorrow but the church of today. And if we don't recognise this and mentor a younger generation we will not have much of a church tomorrow! Mentoring – the incredibly valuable practice of pouring one's life into another person so as to produce another mature disciple of Jesus Christ. Most of the time this is a very effective process; after all, it was time tested by Jesus Himself. But once in a while the mentoring relationship fails to produce its desired result. When the mentor is removed from the equation, the mentee goes down the tubes spiritually.

I think of a relationship between two men. The one man spent years pouring his life into his friend, and so long as he was right there, encouraging, and holding him accountable, everything went pretty well. But when God removed the mentor, it was almost no time before the younger man had backslidden into former habit patterns that were destructive.

I've seen this kind of situation happen elsewhere. Sometimes the stabilising influence is a parent, or a pastor, or a youth worker. So long as that person is prominent in the relationship, the learner seems to stay on the straight and narrow. But when that parent dies, or the pastor leaves, or the youth worker moves on, disaster strikes. That's what happened in our story from 2 Chronicles 23 and 24. The Old Testament King we want to study is Joash, and the epitaph we will use to summarise his life is found in Chapter 24, verse 20: "Because you have forsaken the LORD, He has forsaken you."

We're going to spend a few more paragraphs on the historical background, because we're passing through several generations as we move from Jehoshaphat in our last Chapter to Joash in this – covering the half-century from 850 to 800 BC. But I think you will see the value of it if you keep track with me. Let me spell out the key points.

Jehoram succeeded his father Jehoshaphat.

Jehoshaphat was a good King, by and large, but he failed at his most critical task – parenting. I have some sympathy because I think that the always-difficult task of rearing children must be especially hard for someone with the kind of responsibilities and privileges a king has. I think an argument can be made that the busier a parent is and the more wealth he has at his disposal, the greater the temptation there is to relegate child rearing to others – nannies, sports coaches, private schools, etc. Jehoshaphat had seven sons who grew up with great privilege. He gave them all expensive gifts, but to Jehoram he gave the Kingdom – not because he was the wisest but simply because he was the first-born – probably not a sufficient reason.

Jehoram was married to Athaliah, the daughter of Ahab and Jezebel.

One of Jehoshaphat's greatest weaknesses was his penchant for peace with the Northern Kingdom, which drove him to compromise at several key points in his life. One of the most damaging compromises was his decision to seek a political alliance with Ahab by obtaining Ahab's daughter Athaliah to marry his son Jehoram. This daughter of Jezebel was nearly as wicked as her mother, and just as much of an idol worshiper. Single-handedly she came close to destroying the Southern Kingdom of Judah.

Upon assuming the throne, Jehoram promptly killed all six of his brothers, so as to eliminate any future competition. Just imagine executing the siblings you grew up with until age 32! Now I can understand doing something like that at age 16 (just kidding!), but at 32 you would think they had worked through their adolescent jealousies. But the love of power overwhelmed any sense of family loyalty. Jehoram was punished by God with a lingering illness.

Here is how Jehoram's judgment is described: "After all this, the LORD afflicted Jehoram with an incurable disease of the bowels. In the course of time, at the end of the second year, his bowels came out because of the disease, and he died in great pain." I don't know what this disease was – cancer, or some other chronic ailment – but it was extremely painful and it was fatal. The Scriptures give Jehoram the worst imaginable epitaph a person could receive: "He passed away, to no one's regret."

I have conducted a lot of funerals in my pastoral ministry. Some have been delightful experiences, as tributes and praises poured in from all quarters. At other services, however, I have had little option but to just preach the Word, because there wasn't much good to say about the person – even their loved ones didn't have much to say. But I don't think I've ever done a funeral for a person of whom it could be said, as it was of Jehoram, "he passed away, to *no one's* regret." There was not a single person – not a relative, a palace guard, a cook, or a chambermaid, who missed him. That is sad indeed!

Ahaziah succeeded his father Jehoram

All of the monarchs we are looking at today are from the Southern Kingdom of Judah, but they all had a common fatal attraction for the Northern Kingdom of Israel – that idol-worshiping nation that was on its last legs spiritually. Ahaziah was the youngest son of Jehoram, but he received the throne because all of his brothers were killed by Arab raiders. He was 22 years old when he became King, and he reigned in Jerusalem for only one year. We learn several sad things about him. His mother Athaliah encouraged him in doing wrong. What a tragic epitaph for any mother to bear!

Thankfully, most mothers work overtime to turn their children's paths toward wisdom and integrity. It's almost beyond imagination when once in a while we read in the news about a mother who encourages her daughter to become a prostitute or her son to become a thief or a drug pusher. But that is what Athaliah did, only worse – she encouraged her son to become a pagan idolater and a murderer. She obviously inherited her conscience from her own mother, Jezebel.

Not surprisingly, Ahaziah did evil in the eyes of the Lord

That's what verse 4 tells us. In fact, it goes further, "He did evil in the eyes of the LORD, as the House of Ahab had done, for after his father's death *they* became his advisers, to his undoing." Ahaziah started listening to advice from Israel's ambassadors instead of listening to godly advisors in his own Kingdom of Judah. He died at the hands of Jehu.

Jehu had been commissioned by God to destroy the House of Ahab and was busy executing judgment on Ahab's son and successor in the Northern Kingdom when Ahaziah got caught in the crossfire and Jehu executed him, too.

Athaliah succeeded her son Ahaziah

Suddenly this evil woman found herself in a position to seize the throne. Her husband had killed all his brothers; all of her own sons were dead; so she set herself up as Queen. Imagine a daughter of Ahab and Jezebel sitting on the throne, not of the idolatrous House of Israel, the Northern kingdom, but on the throne of David, the House of Judah! How far the righteous have fallen!

The first thing she did was to try to eliminate any potential competition to the throne. Verse 10 says, "When Athaliah the mother of Ahaziah saw that her son was dead, she proceeded to destroy the whole royal family of the House of Judah." Now remember that Athaliah was the wife of the late King Jehoram and the mother of the late King Ahaziah. If she puts out a contract on Ahaziah's descendants, that means she is bent on murdering her own grandchildren, as well as all other relatives of her late husband and son!

Jehosheba hid her infant nephew Joash in the temple

Jehosheba was King Jehoram's daughter, but apparently not Athaliah's daughter. I assume she was the King's daughter by another marriage, thus Athaliah's stepdaughter. She took one of her nephews, the infant son of Ahaziah and grandson of Queen Athaliah, and hid him, along with a nurse to feed him, so his grandmother couldn't kill him. In fact, this little boy named Joash remained hidden at the Temple of God for six years while Athaliah ruled Judah with a godless cruelty.

By the way, the reason his aunt hid Joash in the Temple was probably that Jehosheba herself was married to the High Priest Jehoiada, who would later play such a major role in the life of Joash.

Joash succeeded his grandmother Athaliah

In the seventh year of Athaliah's reign, as well as the seventh year of Joash's life, Jehoiada the High Priest "showed his strength." As High Priest he was the spiritual leader of the nation, and while that didn't give him any particular political power, he realized that the Kingdom would not survive much longer with Athaliah on the throne. So he marshalled all the strength and influence he could muster, risked his own life, and decided to try to save the nation.

Jehoiada the high priest plotted to crown Joash at age 7

While seven is a pretty young age for anyone to become a king, *any* option was preferable to continuing with a ruler of Athaliah's character. Of course, only a descendent of David was eligible to be king, and that left Joash as the *only* option. The account of the plan devised by the High Priest to bring Joash forth as the new King makes for very interesting reading. In fact, it takes up all of 2 Chronicles 23. Jehoiada involved the priests, the Levites, the army, and the leaders of families – all of whom must have been ripe for a coup against the evil Queen. They crowned Joash, and all the people shouted, "Long live the King! Long live the King!" Athaliah heard the noise and headed for the Temple, where she discovered the whole country bowing down before the boy King.

Ironically Athaliah began protesting, "Treason!" "Treason!" Isn't it interesting how one who is so guilty of treason herself can accuse others of the same deed when they put the *rightful* Ruler on the throne. But her protests were to no avail. Jehoiada was careful, however, not to shed her blood in the Temple – he ordered her put to death on the palace grounds.

Jehoiada made a covenant between the people and God to the effect that "the people and the King would be the LORD's people". A covenant was a public agreement to fulfil a set of requirements in exchange for promised blessings. A public agreement to do something is no guarantee that it's going to be done, but the chances are better than if one merely *says*, "I'm going to do this or that." They are a way of cementing and enforcing the gravity of a decision. And what better covenant to make than one in which believers agree to be God's people! That's even better than agreeing to do godly things.

What does it mean to be God's people? It means to live by God's laws. It means to honour Him with our hearts and actions. It means to worship Him as He desires to be worshiped. Have you ever publicly covenanted to be God's person? When I was growing up it was not uncommon in our circles to have services or special meetings where Christians dedicated their lives to full-time service or re-dedicated their lives to the Lord. There was at times a fair amount of emotionalism connected with some of those decisions, but some of those commitments were lasting and profound.

When five young missionary men were massacred in 1956 by the Auca Indians in Ecuador, literally hundreds of young people offered themselves publicly to take their place in service to God, and many of them actually went to the mission field. Some are retiring now after years of serving God. We should not look lightly on the importance of publicly witnessed covenants.

After the people agreed to be God's people, they immediately began to put legs to their commitment. They went to the temple of Baal, where Athaliah undoubtedly worshiped, and tore it down. They smashed the altars and idols and killed the priest of Baal in front of the altars. And what is the result of this political coup?

The last verse of chapter 23 says, "And all the people of the land rejoiced. And the city was quiet, because Athaliah had been slain with the sword."

That is a lot of background material, but I think it's important to grasp as we turn our attention to the reign of this boy-King, Joash.

Joash does what is right in the eyes of the Lord all the years of Jehoiada the priest.

There's something both very encouraging and very discouraging about that statement which comes directly from 2 Chronicles 24:2. How much better it would have been if the author could have written, "Joash did what was right in the eyes of the Lord all the days of his *own* life." But not so – he only did what was right while Jehoiada was alive.

In the opening verses of Chapter 24 we are informed that Joash enjoys a long reign as King. 40 years – and a large family. This is offered as evidence that God's blessing was on his life, though since he was only seven when he began to reign, that means he died at the young age of 47.

What Joash is best known for is his effort to restore the Temple of Solomon, which had fallen into terrible disrepair in the century since Solomon built it and dedicated it. He first tries to finance this task by urging the priests and Levites to collect the money through a taxation system. "But," according to verse 5, "the Levites did not act at once." That's an understatement if there ever was one, because the parallel passage in 2 Kings tells us that 23 years passed with little or nothing being accomplished. Apparently the Levites were not receiving enough money both to live on and to carry out essential services, and they didn't feel they should also be responsible to raise the huge sums of money needed to restore the Temple. But Joash steps up to the plate and demonstrates some very creative leadership.

He orders a specially made chest to be placed outside the Gate of the Temple. He then issues a proclamation, encouraging everyone to bring to the Lord the tax that Moses had required of Israel in the desert 600 years earlier, but which had since fallen into disuse. Apparently instead of making this tax mandatory, people are encouraged to bring it voluntarily and freely. The result? It says in verse 10: "All the officials and all the people brought their contributions gladly, dropping them into the chest until it was full." Nor does that happen only once. Again and again the chest is filled up, emptied, and then returned again to its place. It says, "They did this regularly and collected a great amount of money." All of the funds go to the repair and reconstruction of the Temple. For the people of Israel the Joash chest became a symbol of generous giving above and beyond the tithe, and it provided all the funds needed to fix the Temple and re-institute regular worship there.

We read in verse 14 that "As long as Jehoiada lived, burnt offerings were presented continually in the Temple of the LORD." But then in the last paragraph of Chapter 24 we read that Jehoiada dies. It shouldn't have been unexpected, for the poor man was really, really old, but few were prepared for the major change that his death would bring upon the nation. It says, "Now Jehoiada was old and full of years, and he died at the age of a hundred and thirty. He was buried with the Kings in the City of David, because of the good he had done in Israel for God and His Temple".

Though this man was never the official ruler of the nation – only the power and influence *behind* the throne – he managed to keep the ship of state headed in the right direction and to keep the young King rightly focused for as long as he lived. However, we read in verse 17: "After the death of Jehoiada, the officials of Judah came and paid homage to the king, and he listened to them." These were the equivalent of lobbyists today, special interest groups who had agendas they wanted the King to follow. Since Jehoiada is no longer around to keep these men away from the King, Joash listens to them. They have persuasive arguments; they have money; they have culture. Why shouldn't he listen to them? But then we learn that, "They abandoned the Temple of the LORD, the God of their fathers, and worshiped Asherah poles and idols." This is amazing to me! After a nearly 25-year obsession with having the Temple repaired, Joash listens to counsellors who have abandoned the Temple of the Lord. And he himself apparently does the same. How do you explain such a turn-around? The only way I can think of is to suggest that he was more interested in the Temple than he was in the Lord of the Temple. I think it is possible for any of us to develop a project-fixation in our walk with God. Get this task done; complete that programme; all the while we are neglecting the development of a close walk with God. Furthermore, Verse 19: "Although the LORD sent prophets to the people to bring them back to Him, and though they testified against them, they would not listen."

One particular prophet is mentioned – Zechariah, the son of Jehoiada the High Priest. He stood before the people and said, "This is what God says: 'Why do you disobey the LORD's commands? You will not prosper. Because you have forsaken the LORD, He has forsaken you'". We simply must realise that we cannot forsake the Lord or abandon his Word with impunity. Everything will not be the same. Tragically, Joash and his counsellors refuse to listen to Zechariah. Verse 21: "But they plotted against him, and by Order of the King they stoned him to death in the Courtyard of the LORD's Temple. King Joash did not remember the kindness Zechariah's father Jehoiada had shown him but killed his son."

Stop and think about what's happening here. If Zechariah is the son of Jehoiada, then he is also the relative of Jehosheba, the very aunt who saved Joash's life years earlier by hiding him in the temple. That would make Zechariah the cousin of Joash. Very possibly these two played together in the confines of the temple in their early years. Now Joash has Zechariah stoned to death in the Courtyard of God's House just because he doesn't take to his warning from God.

Interestingly, Jesus Himself refers to this incident in the New Testament when He denounces the Scribes and Pharisees as snakes and a brood of vipers. The shedding of the innocent blood of Abel is recorded in Genesis the first book of the Old Testament, while Zechariah's innocent blood is recorded in the last book of the Old Testament (the Hebrew Old Testament was in a different order than ours and 2 Chronicles was the last book). In effect Jesus is saying that God will charge those who put Jesus to death with not only the guilt of His execution, but also that of all the innocent victims from Genesis to Revelation! These two murders stand out in God's eyes above and beyond most other heinous sins, and they serve as precursors to the most inexcusable of all deaths – the death of Jesus on the cross.

Here is what Zechariah says as he lay dying: "May the LORD see this and call you to account." The Lord does indeed see it, and within a few months Joash finds himself in a war with Aram. Previously, Jehoshaphat went up against a much larger army, but the Lord gave him a total victory without his army even having to fight. Joash loses his battle, even though his forces outnumber the enemy by a huge margin. Clearly, "It is not by might nor by power, but by my Spirit, says the Lord."

Joash is buried in the city of Jerusalem, but not in the tombs of the Kings. That may not seem like such a big deal to most of us today, because we know that the resting place of the body does not affect the resting place of the spirit, but I'm not sure the ancient Israelites understood that as well. The decision to not allow him to be buried in the tombs of the Kings is a significant expression of shame upon Joash.

Let's get to the principles to ponder and to pursue.

First: The task of mentoring is not done until the disciple is mature in Christ, and, I might add, dependent upon God rather than upon the mentor

Parents, you have not completed your job if all you do is get your child through school sober, as a professing Christian, and still a virgin. If your child is unprepared to stand alone to face the challenges of life away from home, to claim his or her faith as their own, and to stand up to the temptations of an evil culture when mum and dad are not around, then perhaps all you have accomplished is to put a wall of protection, a cocoon, around them for the first 18 years of their lives. A cocoon is a good thing for a developing caterpillar, but once it is ready to metamorphose into a butterfly, that cocoon acts like a prison. The protection of your child is no small accomplishment, but it is not the greatest possible accomplishment. What would be greater is to have brought your child (or anyone you may have nurtured), to a place of spiritual maturity and dependence upon God rather than upon you.

Maybe you teach children at Church or you are a youth worker and you've been able to see your charges survive adolescence in reasonable fashion. Your job is not done until that young person can stand on his or her own and defend his faith and make moral choices when no one is around.

I see a message here as well for those who are being discipled. If you lean too heavily upon your mentor, whoever that may be, if you put that person on a pedestal and imitate him, rather than imitate his faith, you may face a very difficult situation when that person moves away or dies or for some other reason is no longer available to you. Make sure that your faith is not a second-hand faith but a personal faith. Make sure you're not depending too much on your parents or your pastor or your best friend, but rather on God who wants to be your closest mentor and friend. But don't forget, He will become your prosecutor, judge and jury if you go your own way like Joash did.

The epitaph. "If you forsake the Lord, He will forsake you," has a wonderful antidote, found in James 4:8: "Come near to God and He will come near to you." Yes. All who draw near to Him and call on the Name of the Lord will be saved. And not only will they be saved – they will also be given the power to persevere in their walk with the Lord to the end.

Second: It's more important how you end than how you start

Some of you may have got off to a really bad beginning, wasting enormous opportunities, involved in deep sin, and pretty much making a shambles of life. But it's not too late to write a new epitaph. If you're still breathing, you have the opportunity to end well. On the other hand, no matter how great our beginning, if we abandon the Lord and walk away from our covenants, He will say on that Judgment Day, "I never knew you."

May God teach us from the mistakes of Joash to become dependent upon Him rather than our mentors, and to end well. It's not just how you start, it's how you finish.

Chapter 10
Uzziah
Feeling Too Good About Yourself

What do these three individuals have in common? Richard Nixon, Elvis Presley and Jim Bakker? Well, for one thing each one reached the pinnacle of his profession – politics for Nixon, musical entertainment for Presley, and religious television for Bakker. In addition, each one bent the rules. And sadly, each one saw their careers come to a shameful end. I suggest to you that the fatal flaw in each of these men was PRIDE, which is probably best defined in biblical terms as "thinking more highly of oneself than one ought to think." We hear a lot these days about the problem of low self-esteem; in fact, one might be tempted to conclude from a lot of the psychological literature that most of the problems in the world today result from the fact that people don't feel good about themselves. Unfortunately we don't hear nearly as much about inordinate self-esteem, or pride, which the Bible indicates is an even more destructive problem.

In this Chapter we come to Uzziah, King of Judah, who is an example of the tragic consequences of pride: "his pride led to his downfall." Reflect on his relatively brief story from 2 Chronicles 26. For the sake of space, this is just a selection of verses to give you the feel of the passage.

"Uzziah was sixteen years old when he became King, and he reigned in Jerusalem 52 years. He did what was right in the eyes of the LORD, just as his father Amaziah had done. As long as he sought the LORD, God gave him success. God helped him against the Philistines and his fame spread as far as the border of Egypt, because he had become very powerful. Uzziah built. He had people working his fields and vineyards in the hills and in the fertile lands, for he loved the soil. Uzziah had a well-trained army. His fame spread far and wide, for he was greatly helped until he became powerful. But after Uzziah became powerful, his pride led to his downfall. He was unfaithful to the LORD his God, and entered the Temple of the LORD to burn incense on the altar of incense.

Azariah the priest with eighty other courageous priests of the LORD followed him in. They confronted him and said, "It is not right for you, Uzziah, to burn incense to the LORD. That is for the priests, the descendants of Aaron, who have been consecrated to burn incense. Leave the sanctuary, for you have been unfaithful; and you will not be honoured by the LORD God.

Uzziah, who had a censer in his hand ready to burn incense, became angry. While he was raging at the priests in their presence before the incense altar in the LORD's Temple, leprosy broke out on his forehead. King Uzziah had leprosy until the day he died. The other events of Uzziah's reign, from beginning to end, are recorded by the prophet Isaiah son of Amoz.

Uzziah rested with his fathers and was buried near them in a field for burial that belonged to the Kings, for people said, 'He had leprosy.' And Jotham his son succeeded him as King."

Uzziah was only 16 years old when he became King, the second boy-King we have come across in our studies, Joash having reigned from age 7. He was on the throne a total of 52 years, though part of that time he was co-regent with his father and later co-regent with his son. Fifty-two years is an incredibly long time for a person to rule a country. Only Queen Elizabeth approaches Uzziah's tenure in modern times, and, of course, she is a Ruler in name only. We're going to consider Uzziah's life in three parts: His early spiritual credentials. His admirable achievements. His prideful rebellion. Then we will examine the anatomy of pride and conclude with some important biblical principles.

We start with: Uzziah's early spiritual credentials

Our text says of this King that "He did what was right in the eyes of the Lord, just as his father Amaziah had done." At first glance that looks like really good news, because Amaziah and Uzziah are both counted among the 8 godly Kings of Judah (out of 20). But we need to ask what those two words "just as" mean. If Uzziah did what was right in the eyes of the Lord, just as his father Amaziah had done, how well did Amaziah do? In Chapter 25:2 it says, "He did what was right in the eyes of the LORD, but not wholeheartedly." Indeed, that's what we find in Uzziah's story. He followed the same pattern his father followed. Half-hearted commitment to God.

How is your heart? One Pastor said, "I was given a little brass heart that I have since carried every single day in my pocket, along with my change. It reads on one side, 'The Heart of a Leader,' and on the other side, 'Proverbs 4:23: Above all else, guard your heart.' Why? 'For it is the wellspring of life.' Every time I dig in my pocket for money, out comes that reminder, 'Guard your heart.' I need that, because it is so easy to have my heart drawn away from God to material things, and even good things that aren't the best things."

Verse 5 goes on to say, "He sought God during the days of Zechariah, who instructed him in the fear of God." We found a similar situation with Joash, who, we were told, "did what was right in the Eyes of the LORD, all the years of Jehoiada the priest." We noted that when spiritual fruit in a person's life is only observable so long as a mentor or parent or pastor or friend is in the picture, that is an indication that the person has never made the faith his own, never come to real maturity. He has become dependent upon another human being rather than upon God. That seems to be the case also with Uzziah. So long as Zechariah was around, Uzziah sought the LORD. But the implication is that when Zechariah died, the King was left rudderless.

Is there someone in your life who is keeping you on the straight and narrow by virtue of their influence or friendship, but you haven't ever come to point of taking a stand on your own? I suspect there are some husbands reading who are Christians by proxy. What I mean by that is you go to Church because your wife has a relationship with Jesus, and you see what it's done for her and you even like what her faith has done for your home. But you know in your heart that if something happened to her, you would bail out because her faith is not yours. I suspect there are some young people who go to Church because their parents go. And you go off to university. Your stated intentions are to connect with a campus ministry or a local Church, but I'll tell you, those intentions will go nowhere unless you have a faith of your own. The peer pressure or party late on Saturday night will overcome any intentions that aren't grounded in a genuine relationship with Christ. Uzziah and Joash largely had a second-hand faith. That's not good enough when temptations rise and the going gets tough.

Nevertheless, despite these danger signals, King Uzziah started off pretty well and accomplished some pretty incredible things, and the reason is clearly stated in principle form at the end of verse 5: "As long as he sought the LORD, God gave him success."

That, I believe, is a timeless principle that is just as good today as it was in 750 BC. In fact, I do not believe there are any exceptions to it. As long as, but only as long as, we seek the Lord, God will give us success. Of course, to maintain that position, we have to define "success" correctly. Clearly there are people who have sought the LORD but who have not achieved financial success, or musical success, or business success. Success must be defined in biblical terms, and I would like to take a stab at that. "Success, I would say, is achieving the highest purpose for which God created us individually." He knows us better than we know ourselves. He created us and He gifted us. When we use our gifts and talents for the purpose He designed us, then we find success, along with fulfilment and joy.

I know some very successful people in God's eyes who would not be judged particularly successful by many of their peers. The key is to realise that God doesn't promise to give us success as long as we work hard, or earn advanced degrees, or marry well, or eat right. But He does promise to give us success as long as we seek Him. And a large part of what that means is being obedient to this Book the Bible. Read carefully to what the Lord said to Joshua in Joshua 1, Be strong and very courageous. . . Do not let this Book of the Law depart from your mouth; meditate on it day and night, so that you may be careful to do everything written in it. Then you will be prosperous and successful."

Early in his reign young King Uzziah sought the Lord, and the Lord gave him success. He was on his way to becoming not just a good King but a great one. He went to war and God helped him. His army was well trained, well organized, and well equipped.

Uzziah had building interests as we are told that he rebuilt a town and built towers in the desert, presumably to provide protection for travellers and perhaps to serve as outposts for the military. Uzziah "dug many cisterns, because he had much livestock in the foothills and in the plain. He had people working his fields and vineyards in the hills and in the fertile lands, for he loved the soil."

This man Uzziah's achievements were really significant, and they are summarised in verse 8: "His fame spread as far as the border of Egypt, because he had become very powerful," and again in verse 15: "His fame spread far and wide, for he was greatly helped until he became powerful." Clearly the principle that "as long as he sought the LORD, God gave him success" was fulfilled in the life of Uzziah, King of Judah. But then we come to a third chapter in Uzziah's life, a sad chapter. I call it Uzziah's prideful rebellion.

Here too a statement is made that turns out to be a timeless and profound principle: "After he became powerful, his pride led to his downfall." You know, the Scriptures leave no doubt about the dangers of pride and the tragic results of it in a person's life. In Scripture passage after Scripture passage, Old Testament and New, from Satan's rebellion against God before the

Garden of Eden to the Great White Throne Judgment in Revelation, we see the tragic consequences of human pride.

C.S. Lewis writes in *Mere Christianity,* "The essential vice, the utmost evil, is Pride. Unchastity, anger, greed, drunkenness, and all that, are mere fleabites in comparison; it was through Pride that the devil became the devil; Pride leads to every other vice; it is the complete anti-God state of mind. . . . As long as you are proud you cannot know God. A proud man is always looking down on things and people; and, of course, as long as you are looking down, you cannot see something that is above you."

Look at what happened to Uzziah as a result of his pride. It says in verse 16: "He was unfaithful to the LORD his God, and entered the Temple of the LORD to burn incense on the altar of incense." Now we may not think of burning incense in the Temple as a particularly heinous sin, but the issue is not what we think. God had made it explicitly clear that only priests were to burn incense. Uzziah was aware of it. But he thought because he was King he could make his own rules. Worse than that, He persisted in his disobedience even after being warned. You remember the story. Azariah the priest stepped forward with 80 other courageous priests of the Lord and followed Uzziah into the Temple. It took some serious fortitude for these priests to confront the King. In a day and time when the divine right of kings was taken for granted and it was not unusual at all for a King to execute anyone who disagreed with him, these men of God stood up for the truth, no matter what the consequences. But Uzziah persisted in his disobedience, becoming angry with the priests. In fact, he went into a rage. After all, what right did these puny priests have to challenge him, the King? Well, they had no power, for sure, but God did. It says, "While he was raging at the priests in their presence before the incense altar in the LORD's Temple, leprosy broke out on his forehead."

This, of course, was a stunning blow, because leprosy was tantamount to a slow death sentence. And because it was so contagious, the priests hurried him out of the Temple. That wasn't hard to do, for he himself, "was eager to leave, because the LORD had afflicted him." He couldn't wait to get out of there, worried that something worse might happen to him.

He had to leave the Palace and live in isolation in a separate house, apart from his wife and children, his friends, his advisors, and even the servants who made a King's life so pleasant. He was also excluded from the Temple of the LORD. And he effectively lost his power, for Jotham his son was put in charge of the Palace and began to govern the people. And he died a shameful death. At age 68 Uzziah rested with his fathers and was buried near them in a field that belonged to the Kings. He couldn't be buried with them, but only near them, because "He had leprosy."

I want us to turn our attention to the anatomy of pride. How and why does pride lead to a person's downfall?

1 Pride begins with accomplishment, whether perceived or real

Losers are not usually afflicted with pride. It's winners, or at least people who perceive of themselves as winners, who struggle with pride. There's a story told about a woman who came to her pastor confessing the sin of pride. She said to him, "I spend hours looking in a mirror and admiring myself." The pastor said to her, "My dear, yours is not the sin of pride, it's the sin of imagination." We should note that even perceived accomplishment can produce pride.

I think that men are most susceptible to pride in the area of their work, position, and wealth, while women are probably more tempted toward pride in regard to their looks, their relationships, their homes, and their children. But for both, pride begins with accomplishing something significant, being noticed, reaching a goal.

2 Pride takes root when we forget where our success comes from

Success comes from God. We know that, but we forget it. I think that's why the Psalmist speaks to himself and to us with those striking words, "Bless the Lord, O my soul, and forget not all His benefits." I forget people's names.

But the worst possible thing to forget is God's benefits; forget to thank Him for His blessings, forget to give Him the honour He is due. Pride takes root when we forget where our success comes from.

3 Pride causes us to do things we would never do otherwise.

Pride caused Uzziah to take risks, to become reckless, to assume authority he was never given. It always does that. As I have watched the news accounts of CEO's who have looted their companies, I see men who have become bigger than life in their own eyes. They have become a law unto themselves, reckless in their wheeling and dealing and cheating.

Let us bring it a little closer to home. In what ways does pride cause us to take unnecessary risks or to assume authority that hasn't been delegated to us? Many of the affairs I have handled in my counselling with men have had pride at their root. A guy gets a few promotions at work, he earns more money, he discovers that money is power, he begins to believe his own press clippings, and pretty soon he becomes extremely vulnerable. His wife still treats him the way she always did, because she knows he still puts his trousers on one leg at a time. But some woman at the office begins to treat him like a little god. Believe me, he's headed for serious trouble. What kind of behaviour is pride producing in you, behaviour that you wouldn't have considered possible before?

4 Pride demonstrates itself in angry confrontation

I think that what happened to Uzziah with the priests is not unusual at all when a person becomes consumed with pride. The telltale sign of a proud person is that he doesn't listen to those who warn him; instead he becomes angry at their audacity to question him. I think it is a fair rule of thumb that when a person gets very angry upon being confronted, you're dealing with either a very insecure person or a very proud person or both. Humble people can get angry, too; after all, Jesus did. But their anger is generally righteous indignation, anger because the innocent are hurt or justice is being skewed. They don't get angry when they are themselves attacked. Instead they either acknowledge their mistakes and apologise, or they explain themselves and leave it with God. But the proud person lashes back even when he knows in his heart he is wrong.

5 Pride results in destruction and shame

Uzziah reached a sad and tragic end, but it is no different than many today who in their pride decide to go it alone without God. Listen! Pride always results in a fall. That fall may be just a disciplinary action to bring you back to your senses. But it could also result in eternal judgment. If you persist in your pride and disobedience, you will miss out on your only opportunity to receive salvation and spend eternity with God, for that privilege is given only to those who bow the knee to Jesus Christ.

All of this is important. We need to draw some principles out of this before we close the Chapter.

Principle 1: Genuine success in life is always a gift from God

James tells us that: "Every good and perfect gift is from above, coming down from the Father of the heavenly lights." And he means "every."

Principle 2: The Lord who blesses us also disciplines us

There are many today who view God as good and kind; in fact, they look at Him almost as the great Santa Claus in the sky. But God is more than that – much more. He is holy and just. He cannot ignore sin, especially in the lives of His children. So He disciplines us. Hebrews 12 is a powerful passage and brings together the love and discipline of God and essentially tells us we cannot have one without the other.

Listen to these words: "Our fathers disciplined us for a little while as they thought best; but God disciplines us for our good, that we may share in His holiness. No discipline seems pleasant at the time, but painful. Later on, however, it produces a harvest of righteousness and peace for those who have been trained by it" (Hebrews 12:10).

If you are undergoing discipline today, humble yourself now while there is opportunity for repentance and restoration.

Principle 3: The test of prosperity is even more difficult than the test of adversity

I have known what it is to struggle financially, unsure as to what will happen next. At times like that it makes us pray harder and lean more on the Lord. When we had virtually nothing by the world's standards, we had to rely on the Lord because there were no other options. Time and again I remember how God came through for us in miraculous ways. But now there are other options. Trust can be put in material possessions. I'm not sure I have always passed the test. How about you? How are we doing with the test of prosperity?

What is God saying to you through the life of Uzziah, King of Judah? Whatever else you learn, don't let it be said of you that "after you became powerful or popular or wealthy or famous, pride led to your downfall and you were unfaithful to the Lord your God."

Chapter 11
Ahaz
In Time Of Trouble You Crumble

Are you struggling to keep reading this book because you face some trouble today? Are you out of work or facing the strong possibility of unemployment? What about financial problems? Relationship difficulties? Physical issues? Emotional problems? Temptation or even addiction? I suspect nearly everyone is in one kind of trouble or another. Trouble can have various sources. Some is due simply to the fact that we live in a fallen world. Some trouble is due to sin in the lives of others (you can become the innocent victim of a drunk driver, or of a terrorist). Still other troubles can be the result of Satanic attack. There are sufficient examples of this in the Scripture that we ought to be wary and cautious. But let's face it, a great deal of the trouble we get into is directly due to sin in our own lives. This latter category can itself be divided into two parts: the natural consequences of sin and the "discipline" of the Lord. If you're lazy, you're going to be poor; if you smoke for 35 years, you're likely to get cancer. The Lord doesn't have to step in and take any direct action. That's just how He built the universe. But sometimes our sin brings direct action from the Lord.

The entire twelfth chapter of Hebrews is about discipline and the danger of reacting wrongly to it. The author of Hebrews begins by glancing back at the Hall of Faith he has just described in Chapter 11 – the great heroes of the Old Testament – and using those individuals as a gallery of encouragement to us. He offers this exhortation: "Surrounded by such a great cloud of witnesses, let us throw off everything that hinders and the sin that so easily entangles, and let us run with perseverance the race marked out for us."

Hindrances and discouragement are all around us. Trouble is everywhere. We don't even have to go looking for it. But how do we respond? The single most important thing we can do is to keep our eyes fixed on Jesus. Hebrews 12 says, "Let us fix our eyes on Jesus, the author and perfecter of our faith, who for the joy set before Him endured the cross, scorning its shame, and sat down at the right hand of the Throne of God. Consider Him who endured such opposition from sinful men, so that you will not grow weary and lose heart."

Jesus didn't earn trouble because of his own sin – He only endured trouble because of the sin of others. But we *do* earn trouble because of our sin, and verse 4 goes on to address that issue: "In your struggle against sin . . . you have forgotten that word of encouragement that addresses you as sons: 'My son, do not make light of the Lord's discipline and do not lose heart when He rebukes you, because the Lord disciplines those He loves, and He punishes everyone He accepts as a son.'"

Here we are urged to avoid two responses to the Lord's discipline: making light or losing heart. Don't thumb your nose at it, and don't become so discouraged that you give up. You see, the Lord's discipline is a sign of love. In fact, "if you are not disciplined," it goes on to say, "then you are illegitimate children and not true sons." I received a lot of discipline as I was growing up. I remember my dad saying, "I wouldn't do this if I didn't love you," and then he'd let me have it. I always wondered why my parents played favourites and loved me more than the loved my sister. But as difficult as it was to receive the discipline, I knew I needed it, and for the most part I accepted it and learned from it.

We come to a sad story about a wicked King of Judah named Ahaz. He had a key place of leadership among God's people, and because leaders set the standard, God could not ignore his sinful actions and attitudes. So He troubled him. Yet Ahaz never accepted his trouble as discipline, never learned from it, never saw the loving hand of God behind it. His reaction was to simply sin more.

2 Chronicles 28 says of Ahaz, "In his time of trouble King Ahaz became even more unfaithful to the Lord."

Discipline, in contrast to punishment, is always designed for correction; its purpose is to get the person's attention, change him for the better, and restore him to usefulness. When we respond appropriately to the Lord's discipline, tremendous good can result. But if we respond to the Lord's discipline with further unfaithfulness, the results are tragic. In fact, there no longer remains any hope for such a person. How can there be? After all, if a person ignores or rejects the very means God designs to bring them to their senses, what do we expect God to do? Force them to repent? This He will not do.

My approach will be to briefly state the sad but fascinating story of Ahaz and then ask the question, "How do *we* respond to the discipline of the Lord?"

Just a brief comment about the historical background.

Ahaz was 20 when he became King of Judah and he reigned for 16 years. His father was Jotham, and his grandfather was Uzziah. Uzziah was a King who started out well, but he didn't have a whole heart for God and his pride led to his downfall. His son Jotham had to take over the royal duties when Uzziah became a leper. Jotham saw the awful consequences of sin in his father's life, and he made sure he didn't make the same mistakes. When Jotham died of unknown causes at the age of 41, his son Ahaz succeeded him at the age of 20, and he reigned in Jerusalem sixteen years.

Probably the most far-reaching historical event in Ahaz' life is one that is not even mentioned in 2 Chronicles 28 but only in 2 Kings 17: The

Kingdom of Israel was destroyed by the Assyrians while Ahaz was on the Throne of Judah. The importance of this event is that despite the destruction and demise of his countrymen to the north, which occurred right before his eyes, Ahaz refused to repent of his own wickedness. He refused to believe that God would dare do to Judah what He had done to Israel. Eventually that's exactly what happened.

Now the opening paragraph of 2 Chronicles 28 paints a startling picture of the detestable apostasy of Ahaz. Heresy is a departure from correct teaching in some important area; apostasy is total departure from the faith. A heretic is a believer whose theology is screwed up in some area or other. An apostate is an unbeliever who was once identified with and immersed in the faith but abandoned it. Ahaz was an apostate.

Ahaz did not have the whole heart for God that his ancestor David had. He did not even have the half-heart that his grandfather and great-grandfather had; he had no heart for God. In fact, it says in verse 2 that he walked in the ways of the Kings of Israel. He took the Northern Kingdom, which didn't have a single godly King in over 200 years of history, as the pattern for his behaviour. Furthermore, he actually got into the business of manufacturing idols. He offered his own sons as child sacrifices to pagan gods. And he set up worship centres everywhere *except* at the Temple, which was the one place God called the people to worship. Frankly, he was the worst of all the Kings of Judah.

God couldn't just ignore this behaviour and remain true to Himself, so beginning in verse 5 we read that God engineered Judah's defeat by Aram and Israel, resulting in 120,000 casualties. The fact that these defeats were not just bad luck is made very clear in the text: "Therefore the LORD his God handed him over to the king of Aram . . . He was also given into the hands of the King of Israel, who inflicted heavy casualties on him."

This defeat was especially painful to Ahaz because three of the casualties were individuals very close to him. One was his own son, another the officer in charge of his Palace, and a third was his closest aide. But even more devastating for the nation was the fact that prisoners numbering 200,000 were seized, plus a great deal of plunder. The captives were primarily women and children. Imagine the turmoil in Judah when the magnitude of this defeat was realized. Wouldn't the anger and resentment of his fellow-countrymen, if not the knowledge that the Lord was disciplining him, drive Ahaz to his knees? Well, we're left in suspense on that question for a moment as the writer of Chronicles takes a strange detour to tell us about a prophet who comes and brings a strong warning from God. But he doesn't come to warn Ahaz or Judah but rather the Northern Kingdom of Israel!

Now to make sense of this story, we must keep in mind that God's chosen people, the Israelites, whose first three Kings were Saul, David, and Solomon, had undergone a civil war after Solomon's reign and had split into two nations–the Northern Kingdom of Israel and the Southern Kingdom of Judah. None of Israel's Kings were descendants of David and none of them were godly. All of Judah's Rulers were descendants of David (except for the brief reign of Athaliah), and eight of them were godly, or partially so. But right now Judah has a King who is as ungodly as any King of Israel. Because of his sin, God is disciplining him, and God is using the godless Nation of Israel to bring judgment on Ahaz and Judah. But what we discover is the surprising repentance of Israel, the Northern Kingdom. The prophet Oded challenged them to return their prisoners.

Amazingly, the leaders of Israel recognised their guilt and repented. They confronted those arriving from the war and said, "You must not bring those prisoners here or we will be guilty before the LORD. Do you intend to add to our sin and guilt? For our guilt is already great, and His fierce anger rests on Israel." The soldiers responded by giving up their prisoners and their plunder. Not only that, they clothed all the prisoners who were naked, they provided them with shoes, food, drink, and medicine; those that were weak were put on donkeys; and they even *took* them back, rather than *send* them back to their homeland.

Please grasp the significance of all this. The reason the writer of Chronicles is focusing our attention on this unprecedented turn-around by the godless Nation of Israel (admittedly temporary) is to contrast it with the reaction of Ahaz, King of the supposedly godly Nation of Judah. What was that reaction? In verse 16 the writer turns back to Ahaz and notes for us his further apostasy. Before he had only been unfaithful; now he was most unfaithful. What is the evidence? The focus of his unfaithfulness is his decision to go to Assyria for help instead of to the Lord. Time and again the Lord had warned His people not to trust in alliances with other nations but to turn to Him in time of trouble. But Ahaz turned to Assyria instead. Verse 20 tells us that "Tiglath-Pileser King of Assyria came to him, but he gave him trouble instead of help." Isn't that always the result when we try to solve our problems using human manipulations instead of divine solutions. Ahaz is a slow learner if there ever was one.

He tries to buy off the King of Assyria by taking some of the treasures from the Temple of the Lord (apparently gold fixtures and other valuable articles), plus other treasures from the Palace and from the royal family, and giving them to the King, "but that did not help him." It is at this point that we read Ahaz' epitaph: "In his time of trouble King Ahaz became even more unfaithful to the LORD." Believe it or not, he began to offer sacrifices to the Assyrian gods. Here is his reasoning, found in verse 23: "Since the gods of the Kings of Aram have helped them, I will sacrifice to them so they will help me. But they were his downfall and the downfall of all Israel (Northern and Southern kingdoms)." This was a pagan altar, mind you. But Ahaz wasn't satisfied to simply *add* a pagan altar, for the passage goes on to say that he ordered the priest to *remove* from the Temple the bronze altar, as well as the rest of the furnishings that had been in the Temple since Solomon's day – all "in deference to the King of Assyria." Then he shut and sealed the doors of the Lord's Temple. He put up a "closed" sign on the Temple and instead set up altars on every street corner in Jerusalem. Then he spread his idolatry to every town in Judah.

Verse 24 of 2 Chronicles 28 closes his reign with this observation: he "provoked the LORD, the God of his fathers, to anger." And he died, but was not buried with the Kings because his wickedness had brought reproach and shame to his memory. So far I have pretty much just taught the historical facts surrounding Ahaz King of Judah. I want us now to apply this account to our own lives. I want us to focus on our response to trouble, particularly the kind that is brought upon us by our own behaviour. This story drives us to consider a different question, "Why do bad things happen to bad people?" For some reason we even struggle with that question. How should guilty people respond to trouble? Or, to bring it all the way home, how do we respond to the discipline of the Lord? As I thought this through, I came up with some common responses I have seen either in my own life or in the lives of Christian people around me.

Some people just don't seem to have a clue as to why they are in trouble, even though it's pretty obvious to others that they've brought it on themselves. They just bemoan their bad luck or stew in their juices, but the thought of actually dealing with the sin that got them where they are never enters their minds. And some people when they experience deserved trouble get angry with God, or blame others, or just play the victim thing to the hilt. When their marriage falls apart or one of their kids goes off the deep end, they are a lot quicker to ask, "God, why didn't you come through for me? Where was my Pastor when I needed him?" than they are to ask, "Where did I fail to love my spouse or train my children? Did I sell my soul to the company while my family went down the toilet?"

Some people simply lose heart as troubles pile up. They know their particular troubles started with disobedience and for a while they worked on the issues, but their efforts weren't successful. This is especially true when people are struggling with an addiction – maybe gambling or alcohol or drugs or sex. They know that behaviour is self-destructive, even suicidal. But every effort to stop has failed and now their hearts are filled with fear and they believe they are hopeless. They feel they are condemned to a life of failure and therefore trouble. That's a lie from the pit of hell. No one is hopeless so long as God is on the throne and so long as He's in the business of redeeming sinful people.

The problem for a lot of people whose lives are really messed up is that we have separated addictions from morality. Alcoholism and gambling and sexual addiction are now viewed as diseases, not sins, in our society. What have we gained by that? Well, we've relieved a lot of people of guilt. What have we lost? We've taken away the only chance many of them have to find complete forgiveness and healing. After all, a disease doesn't need to be forgiven – it just needs to be treated. But when a disease has its roots in sin, treatment can only deal with the symptoms, and often not even those very well; nothing is done with the root of the problem.

Don't misunderstand me. I accept that alcoholism is a disease, and many other addictions may be as well, but they are not exactly like other diseases. They are diseases inextricably tied to bad choices. You can get cancer without anyone committing a sin or making a bad choice. But you can't become addicted without someone making wrong choices, and it's usually the addict himself or herself who makes those choices. Thus to deal with the problem thoroughly we not only have to treat the symptoms, we also have to find forgiveness for the sin. Frankly, once the sin is dealt with, the treatment of the symptoms is a whole lot easier.

The main thing I want to communicate is, don't give up. Don't allow fear and hopelessness to overcome you. If you're going through trouble because of your behaviour, the same God who is disciplining you has the power to heal you, if you will allow Him to. That healing starts with acknowledging that you are a sinner and you can't help yourself.

The first steps on the road to recovery starts right there. But then you must move to the fact that there is One who can help you, and His name is Jesus. He died on the cross for your sins and He offers you forgiveness if you will put your faith and trust in Him.

This was Ahaz' answer, but it's the most tragic response of all.

Every once in a while I come across a professing Christian who takes Ahaz' path. He sins, he is disciplined by the Lord, and in effect he responds, "I don't care. I'm going to do it my way." I know a man who was a lay pastor. He had an affair and divorced his wife. Some time later he came to church, admitted his sin and asked for another chance. He was given another chance, but he had a lot of anger toward the people in his previous church and the way they had treated him. It became obvious that he was having another affair. Today he is living with this other woman, not involved in church at all, and to the best of my knowledge has abandoned the faith.

Do you know how dangerous it is to respond to trouble with further unfaithfulness? If you're feeling the conviction of the Holy Spirit, I can say with confidence that you have *not* completely fallen away. There is still time for you to repent,

Which brings us to the final possible reaction to discipline

This is the only one that makes any long-term sense. Ahaz refused to go this route, and his name is written in infamy as one of the worst leaders of God's people ever. But there are many in Scripture who responded to the trouble that God's discipline brought in their lives with repentance and restoration, and, as a result, they are in God's Hall of Faith in Hebrews 11. There's Noah and Abraham, Jacob and Moses – scoundrels all. There's Samson – talk about a man whose behaviour brought discipline from the Lord! He had his eyes plucked out and had to do the work of a draft horse in a filthy dungeon! There's David who broke five of the ten commandments in one fell swoop, leaving a woman pregnant, her husband dead, his own son dead, and a nation in mourning. But their names are all there because they responded with repentance and God restored them.

Thankfully, God's Hall of Faith was not closed with the end of the Old Testament, for there was room for Peter and the rest of the Apostles, Mary Magdalen and Joseph of Arimethea, and Paul. It wasn't even closed with the end of the

New Testament, for there's room also for Tom, Dick and Harry . . . and you and I.

May it never be said of us, "In time of trouble he or she became even more unfaithful," but rather "In time of trouble he repented. She humbled herself before the Lord. He confessed. She sought forgiveness. He was restored. She became useful once more to a gracious God."

Chapter 12
Judah
A Point Of No Return

I stepped into the hotel lift and pushed the button for my desired floor. As I waited I wondered to myself, "When is this thing going to start moving." Suddenly the door opened and I realised I had moved several flights down without even knowing it. There was no sound to indicate I was moving. There was not a jolt to indicate I had started moving. And there was not a bump at the end to indicate I had been moving. I didn't realise I was moving. I've noticed the same thing to be true in other areas of life.

There was a day when most television programmes were family based and for the most part wholesome. Other than my regular Saturday night ritual of trying to out-draw Marshall Matt Dillon at the beginning of Gunsmoke I rarely saw killing. Miss Kitty was apparently the Marshall's girlfriend, but if anything inappropriate ever happened no one ever knew it. (It was not until many years later that I understood what Miss Kitty did for a living.) I did not realise that we had moved but things have changed. Many of the regulars in prime-time programming today make no pretence of the lead characters lack of morality. More often than not the lack of morals is praised and glorified. We were moving, but we are only now beginning to realise how fast and far we were moving.

There was a day when professional athletes and coaches felt an obligation to their fans to be men and women of integrity, at least publicly. If they were guilty of adultery, drunkenness, any form of immorality they would have tried to keep their deeds of darkness in the dark. No longer.

There was a day when things were simpler and or so it seemed. There was a day when one word in 'Gone With the Wind' caused a scandal. Now, movies are filled with curse words and vulgarity, are praised as being "true to life." We are moving but we do not seem to notice.

The elevator in the hotel was so fast and smooth that I moved from floor to floor without noticing. We tend to do the same thing in life. We must be careful that we do not drift into areas that are not healthy without realising it. Be careful of the drift. Are you aware that you are moving? There's no question we are as a nation.

What happens to a nation whose leaders fail to set a high spiritual standard, and thus it abandons its spiritual foundation, pursues false worship, perverts justice, and practices every conceivable kind of sin? In this final Chapter we are going to see the answer to that question.

Remember, we have called this book 'Reigning In Life', because the New Testament tells us that there isn't anything written in the Old

Testament redundant for us. We are called as believers to 'reign in life'. Sometime we are more reigned *over* than reigning. There are practical lessons to learn from the Kings of the Old Testament.

Our final epitaph is not that of a king or a prophet, but rather of a people – the Nation of Judah. It comes from 2 Chronicles 36:16, but I have shortened it in order to get it on the tombstone. Let me read you the full epitaph: "They mocked God's messengers, despised His words, and scoffed at His prophets until the wrath of the LORD was aroused against His people and there was no remedy." But thankfully the grave that is marked by this tombstone turns out not to be Judah's final resting place. Due solely to the grace and mercy of God, the notice of Judah's demise was premature, as I will explain.

I think it would be profitable to take a quick overview of Jewish history, so we can see once again how this portion of history fits into the whole.

The father of the Jewish people was Abraham, who lived in the 21st century BC. He was the first of four great patriarchs – Abraham, Isaac, Jacob and Joseph – who spanned roughly 400 years.

Joseph, the last of the patriarchs, was sold by his brothers into slavery in Egypt and, by God's amazing providence, eventually became the

Prime Minister. Years later, when a great famine hit the entire Middle East, Joseph's brothers went to Egypt to find food and ended up finding something better – reconciliation with their long-lost brother, whom they presumed was dead. Joseph persuaded the Pharaoh to give them a new home in the Nile Delta of Egypt, with the result that this extended family of about 70 members prospered there and became a nation of several million over the next 400 years.

Over time, however, the fortunes of the Israelites declined markedly; they became slaves rather than guests. The Israelites were rescued from Egypt by God's miraculous power. Moses led them across the Sea of Reeds, to Mount Sinai, and then through the desert to the doorstep of the Promised Land.

Tragically, the people rebelled against God and, as a result, they had to spend nearly 40 years wandering in the desert until an entire generation died off. But eventually Joshua led the new generation across the Jordan River and into the land God had promised to Abraham some 700 years earlier.

The Conquest of the land from the pagan tribes who lived there took about 30 years, and then for about 3 centuries the Israelites lived in a sort of theocracy, with God ruling through a series of judges. Eventually they begged God for a king. Why? Because the other nations had one. God reluctantly gave in to their wishes, but He warned them that there were grave dangers associated with centralised power. He gave them Saul as their first King, a man with great potential, but one who failed miserably to live up to his gifts and abilities. He was followed by David, and David by Solomon. This was known as the Golden Age of Israel or the United Monarchy.

The Kingdom split after the death of Solomon, with ten tribes forming the Nation of Israel and two tribes forming the Nation of Judah. Both countries largely failed to follow the Lord, though Judah, whose Kings were all descendants of David, had at least a few good rulers – about 8 out of 20. Israel didn't have a single one, and as a result God brought the Assyrians in to destroy their nation and carry off its people into exile.

To this day they are known as the Ten Lost Tribes of Israel, for no Jewish person today can trace his or her ancestry to any of these tribes. Judah lasted for another 140 years until the Babylonians put it out of its misery.

We will examine the years immediately preceding that awful event, as well as some amazing things that followed. The continuing decline of the nation of Judah, 2 Chronicles 36:1-14.

Josiah was the last good King. While he was just a teenager he launched his greatest work for God. He was able to make such a difference as a leader that the Lord postponed the judgment He had planned on Judah for nearly another generation. Let me just summarise the life of Josiah with a marvellous passage from 2 Kings 23: "Neither before nor after Josiah was there a King like him who turned to the LORD as he did – with all his heart and with all his soul and with all his strength, in accordance with all the Law of Moses. Nevertheless, the LORD did not turn away from the heat of his fierce anger, which burned against Judah because of all that Manasseh (Josiah's grandfather) had done to provoke Him to anger. So the LORD said, "I will remove Judah also from my presence as I removed Israel, and I will reject Jerusalem, the City I chose, and this Temple, about which I said, 'There shall my Name be.'"

In the year that Josiah died, the world stage was in a great state of flux. The Assyrian Empire was in rapid decline. Egypt, which had been a dominant world power for 3000 years, was also in decline. The King of Egypt, went to the aid of the Assyrians to slow down the Babylonians, and Judah was trapped in the middle between these world powers on the north, south, and east. God, of course, was the one really moving the pieces on the chessboard, and He had determined that for a while, at least, Babylon would win.

There were four more Kings of Judah following Josiah – three of his sons and one of his grandsons. Two of them reigned 11 years each, two reigned for three months each, but all four had the same epitaph. Regarding each one we read the exact same words: "He did evil in the eyes of the Lord."

Let's briefly examine each of them. Jehoahaz, also known as Shallum, was the middle son of Josiah but was elevated to the throne before his older brother when Josiah died in battle with the King of Egypt. He reigned only 3 months before being carried off to Egypt as a prisoner, where he died as predicted by the prophet Jeremiah. In Jehoahaz' place the King of Egypt put the eldest son of Josiah on the Throne. His name was Eliakim but it was changed to Jehoiakim, indicating that he was little more than a puppet of Egypt. During Jehoiakim's eleven-year reign the balance of power in the Middle East shifted dramatically from Egypt to Babylon.

Less than three years into Jehoiakim's reign, the new head of the Babylonian Empire, Nebuchadnezzar, soundly defeated the Egyptians. In an effort to extend his control, he forced Jerusalem into submission, seizing tribute and hostages, among whom were Daniel and his friends.

The prophet Jeremiah showed disdain for Jehoiakim by declaring that he would have "the burial of a donkey – dragged away and thrown outside the gates of Jerusalem."

The particular action which prompted this prediction was Jehoiakim's construction of a new Palace, squandering state funds at a time of national crisis. Furthermore, when Jeremiah wrote a scroll of warnings about the coming Judgment of God, Jehoiakim cut up Jeremiah's book and burned it. But just as Jeremiah predicted, Nebuchadnezzar returned to Jerusalem.

More hostages were seized, including Jehoiakim himself, who was bound with bronze shackles for transport to Babylon, but he died in Jerusalem before he could be carried away. Nebuchadnezzar also stripped the Temple of God of all the articles of value (remember, there was more gold in this building than in any other in ancient history) and took it all to his temple in Babylon. Jehoiachin, the 18-year-old son of Jehoiakim and therefore the grandson of Josiah, then became King, but he lost no time demonstrating his own evil heart.

Jeremiah also prophesied against him. Jehoiachin reigned only three months and ten days before King Nebuchadnezzar deposed him and took him as a hostage to Babylon, along with the Queen Mother, princes, and 10,000 leading citizens, including the prophet Ezekiel. In Jehoiachin's place Nebuchadnezzar appointed his uncle (the third son of Josiah) to be King over Judah and changed his name from Mattaniah to Zedekiah. Zedekiah was twenty-one when he became King and managed to survive for eleven years. However, his reign was characterised by continual agitation and unrest in the nation. Some false prophets claimed that God had already broken the yoke of Babylon and that within two years Judah's captives would return home, but Jeremiah denounced them and urged continued submission to Babylon.

Tragically Zedekiah listened to the false prophets and joined a coalition against Babylon. Because of this rebellion, Nebuchadnezzar came to Jerusalem for the third and final time and laid siege to the city. During the 18 months of the siege Jeremiah suffered great hardship at the hands of his fellow countrymen. They considered him a traitor for predicting that Babylon would crush Jerusalem. Zedekiah gave him some half-hearted support, but his officials beat Jeremiah, imprisoned him in a dungeon, and eventually threw him into a mud-filled cistern, but he never stopped speaking the truth.

Jeremiah chapter 39 describes in detail the fall of Jerusalem, including the fact that Zedekiah was captured by Nebuchadnezzar, who slaughtered the sons of Zedekiah before his eyes and then put his eyes out, bound him with bronze shackles, and took him to Babylon. Just imagine living the rest of your life with the last visual image being the execution of your own children!

As we consider the fall of Judah and Jerusalem, I want us to focus upon 2 Chronicles 36:15-23.

God's patience and pity is mentioned

"The LORD, the God of their fathers, sent word to them through his messengers again and again, because He had pity on His people and on His dwelling place." Discipline from the Lord is always preceded by patience. For over 300 years God had worked with this nation. He tried everything imaginable to bring them back to Himself. He gave them blessings, He gave them hardships; He tried pleasure and He tried pain; at times He saturated them with prophetic truth, while at other times He let them try to figure things out on their own. Nothing worked. As a result, God's righteous anger was stirred up.

Verse 16 says, "But they mocked God's messengers, despised His words and scoffed at His prophets until the wrath of the LORD was aroused against His people and there was no remedy." I am aware that God's anger is not a popular concept today, but it is an absolutely essential aspect of His character. A God who did not get angry at the sin of His people would be of no more value than a wife who did not get angry at her husband's philandering.

"God handed all of them over to Nebuchadnezzar." This is not bad luck; this is not even a failure of military preparedness; this is divine discipline. Judah and Jerusalem are no more. But wait! God's incredible mercy always has the last word. That mercy is revealed to us through one of the most amazing prophecies in Scripture.

Once again I turn your attention to the man of God known as the weeping prophet, Jeremiah.

He survived the Babylonian assault on Jerusalem. In fact, he was treated quite well by Nebuchadnezzar and was allowed to remain in the City after the Babylonians left. He wrote a letter to the exiles back in Babylon, encouraging them to settle down, because they were going to be there for a long time. In fact, he told them to pray for Babylon, because if it prospered, they would prosper. But, Jeremiah went on to say, they were not going to be there permanently. "When seventy years are completed for Babylon, I will come to you and fulfil my gracious promise to bring you back to this place."

Fast forward about sixty seven years. Jeremiah is long gone but his prophecy is being read by another of God's prophets. Daniel is now an old man of perhaps eighty or more. He had been taken hostage as a teenager and had lived ever since in Babylon, serving a series of Babylonian Kings, with exceptional competence and faithfulness to the Lord. Then suddenly the City of Babylon fell before the armies of Cyrus and a new world power emerged – the Medes and the Persians. In the first year of Cyrus King of Persia, in order to fulfil the Word of the LORD spoken by Jeremiah, the LORD moved the heart of Cyrus King of Persia to make a proclamation throughout his realm and to put it in writing. This is what Cyrus King of Persia says: "The LORD, the God of Heaven, has given me all the kingdoms of the earth and He has appointed me to build a Temple for Him at Jerusalem in Judah. Anyone of His people among you – may the Lord his God be with him, and let him go up."

The next Book of the Bible, Ezra, begins right at that point by telling the story of how the Jewish people were allowed to return to their land in order to rebuild the Wall, the City, and eventually the Temple. God's incredible mercy was such that He simply could not abandon His people, even after their complete abandonment of Him.

I close with some brief lessons for God's people today that come not only from the epitaph of Judah but also from this whole series of events.

1 We must not presume upon His patience

Every time we sin wilfully, violating the revealed Will of God, we are presuming upon God's patience. Whenever we say to ourselves, "I know God forbids this, but I also know He's a God of grace, so I'm sure He'll forgive me," we are presuming upon His grace. This we must not do. To err is human, I am aware of that. We will never reach a state of perfect holiness in this life. But it is one thing to sin; it is another to have a rebellious attitude and sin wilfully.

2 We must not underestimate His anger

God hates sin. He hates it because it violates all He stands for, but He also hates it because He knows how much it harms us. God isn't just displeased with sin; He isn't just irritated by it; He hates it to the point that He must do something about it, namely discipline His children when they sin.

3 We must not chafe under His discipline

The discipline of the Lord is never pleasant. But the worst thing we can do when disciplined is what King Ahaz did. Remember? In time of trouble he became even more unfaithful. If we react to God's discipline with more sin and more rebellion, we are destroying any chance we have for forgiveness and restoration.

4 We cannot but marvel at His mercy

"Who is a pardoning God like thee?" asks the hymn writer, "Or who has grace so rich and free?" The obvious answer is, "No one!" A God who would bring the rebellious and sinful Israelites back home from Babylon, is also a God who will accept you back from wherever you may have wandered. It's time to turn round, it's time to come home. God loves you. Jesus died for you. He offers you forgiveness for your sins and life forever with Him. Won't you say "yes" to his free offer of salvation?

The train left Colombo, the Capital of Sri Lanka, at 7:30 in the morning, headed for a popular resort area along the Indian Ocean. The train never made it. It was suddenly hit by a massive wall of water – the killer tsunami that devastated so much of South Asia in December of 2004. The force of the waves tore the wheels off some carriages and levelled the train in a grove of palm trees. In one of those countless heart-wrenching scenes that came out of the tsunami aftermath, one young man at the train site wept in the arms of his friends as the body of his girlfriend was buried. He spoke out to this sweetheart who had died on that train: "We met in university. Is this the fate we hoped for?" Then, as he began to sob even more, he said, "My darling, you were the only hope for me."

It's hard to think of a more devastating feeling than losing what you had put all your hopes in. It's a feeling you may know if you've lost your health, the love of your life, your job, an anchor person in your life, the thing you've invested so much in, the thing – or the person – that's been the glue holding your life together. I have friends who have been told by their marriage partner of decades, "I don't love you anymore." When I asked one of those friends how he was doing, he just said, "I'm crushed."

So many of us have either lost – or will lose – someone or something that we had put a lot of our hopes in. Hope is snatched away by death, by divorce, by desertion, by disease, by disaster. Suddenly, our life is thrown into confusion and anxiety and even despair. What we need is something to put our hope in that is never lost – something that can't be touched by death or disease, by divorce, by disaster; something that will never desert us. Actually, someone who will never desert us. Surprisingly, many people have discovered that in losing the source of their hope, they finally found the one hope you can never lose. It could happen to you.

The only life-anchor, the only life-hope you can never lose is a personal love-relationship with God. God alone. Not a religion, but a relationship. It's possible to have a lot of religion and totally miss the relationship with God that you were made for. Any hope we get from anyone or anything on earth is just an unsatisfying substitute for belonging to God. When you belong to Him and you know you do, your soul finally can find rest. But until you belonging to God, your soul is restless.

The hope you've lost, and the emptiness you feel, can lead you today to the hope you'll never lose.

His name is Jesus.

Good News Broadcasting Association (UK)
Back Lane Ranskill DN22 8NN England
info@gnba.net www.gnba.net

Printed in the United Kingdom
by Lightning Source UK Ltd.
114041UKS00001BA/70-81

9 781846 853524